CW00573456

Zodiac Types

This is a Parragon Book
This edition published in 2002

Parragon
Queen Street House
4 Queen Street
Bath BA1 1HE, UK

ISBN: 0-75258-246-1

A copy of the CIP data for this book is available from the British
Library upon request.

The right of Stella Cross to be identified as the author of this work
has been asserted in accordance with Section 77 of the Copyright,
Designs and Patents Act of 1988.

Editorial, design and layout by Essential Books, 7 Stucley Place,
London NW1 8NS

Printed and bound in China

Zodiac Types

Stella Cross

Contents

Introduction   5

Aries   7

Taurus   22

Gemini   37

Cancer   53

Leo   68

Virgo   83

Libra   98

Scorpio   113

Sagittarius   129

Capricorn   144

Aquarius   159

Pisces   175

Further reading   190

Astrology websites   191

Introduction

Most of us know our Sun sign, although we often call it our star sign. In fact, they're one and the same. Our Sun sign is the sign that the Sun occupied at the time of our birth. The term 'star sign' is a reference to the twelve constellations in the zodiac. However, this can be rather misleading!

The astrology practised in the West is more concerned with planets than stars. It focuses on the eight planets in our solar system (Mercury, Venus, Mars, Jupiter, Saturn, Uranus, Neptune and Pluto), plus the Sun and the Moon, which it also considers to be planets. Astrologers are well aware that these aren't really planets and that calling them such gives sceptics instant ammunition! Yet terminology doesn't affect the astrological influence of these very important heavenly bodies.

The zodiac is an elliptical belt of sky around the Earth that contains the twelve constellations – Aries, Taurus, Gemini, Cancer, Leo, Virgo, Libra, Scorpio, Sagittarius, Capricorn, Aquarius and Pisces. Every year, from our vantage point on Earth, the Sun appears to move through each constellation in turn, spending about thirty days in each one. So when the Sun journeys through Leo, babies born at that time will have a Leo Sun sign.

This book is a simple introduction to the twelve Sun signs, describing their general characteristics, how they behave in love, their career potential, the way they handle money and how they can stay healthy. There is also a list of places and objects ruled by each sign, and descriptions of how each sign gets on with the other members of the zodiac. At the end of the book, you'll find a list of other astrology books you might enjoy and some astrology websites to visit.

ARIES

21 March – 20 April

Aries

The Aries Personality

It's hard to ignore an Arien! They have bags of personality and vitality, making them the sort of people who like to be noticed. They hate the thought of taking a back seat in life and will do anything to prevent it. And no wonder, because they belong to the first sign of the zodiac, which means it is natural for them to be leaders, not followers. The last thing any self-respecting Arien wants to do is carry out other people's orders or be at their beck and call. They loathe the thought of just being one of the crowd – instead, they like to adopt a dynamic and adventurous approach to life, and this doesn't change as they get older. They have to be in control of situations; they don't like it one bit when it's the other way round.

Being the first sign of the zodiac makes Ariens instinctively put themselves first. It's as natural to them as breathing. Even if their second thought concerns their nearest and dearest, their first thought will always revolve around themselves. There are degrees of this, of course.

Aries

Occasionally, you may well meet a very selfish Arien who apparently doesn't realize that anyone else in the world exists. They're completely wrapped up in themselves and usually end up all alone. However, the vast majority of Ariens are merely slightly self-centred. Once you understand this, you can work round it.

Life is very black and white for Ariens, with no half measures. That's partly because they belong to the Fire element, which gives them their infectious enthusiasm and adventurous spirit. The other reason is that this sign is ruled by the fiery planet Mars, which stamps its imprint on Ariens by making them short on temper and long on enthusiasm. They're very idealistic and always have high expectations that things will turn out well. As a result, they often do. Mars also gives them plenty of determination and a burning desire to achieve the things they set out to do. An Arien without a goal is a sad sight, because they feel lost without anything to aim for. If their life shrinks so much that they have little to live for, they can become irritable and scratchy over the tiniest snag. It's as though their anger is leaking out in all directions.

Ariens easily lose their tempers but it's all over in a flash. One minute they're shouting their heads off and the next they've forgotten all about it. The only problem is the Arien bluntness – these people like to tell it how it is, and that can lead to hurt feelings when they go too far and don't realize the impact of what they're saying. Life would be much easier for Ariens if they could curb their outspokenness. But then that would take so much fun out of things!

Love

Love and romance are central to an Arien's life. They are idealists, always hoping for a fairytale romance. But they also love the thrill of the chase, and some Ariens find this is the most exciting part of any relationship. They cool off once they get what they want! The Arien's generous spirit and warm personality make them a wonderful friend and a delightful lover. Sex is very important to them because it helps them to work off their abundant energy and also enables them to express their emotions in loving actions; they're demonstrative at the best of times, and enjoy a very physical relationship with their lover. They won't be at all happy if their partner is not as passionate as they are.

Ariens have tremendous faith in other people and this means they always put the utmost trust in their friends and loved ones. When they fall in love (which happens easily, probably more often than they care to admit), they invest everything in their lover, and make a gift of their heart and affections. An Arien's partner holds their lover's fate and happiness in their hands, and with luck nothing will go wrong. However, most Ariens have their hearts shattered at some point in their lives by someone who fails to live up to their expectations.

Is this just one of those things or do Ariens somehow contribute to the situation? They certainly tend to put loved ones on lofty pedestals, believing that they can do no wrong. Everything's great while their loved one occupies this high position, but the moment they turn out to be human after all the Arien feels disappointed and crushed. How could they have been let down like this? If this person really causes the Arien a lot of pain, they'll never feel the same way about them again and it'll hurt like mad. Does it make the Arien more wary in future? No, not really! They find it very hard to learn from their mistakes and will often repeat them over and over again.

Career

Ariens are free spirits, which means they can't abide any sort of job that ties them down or restricts their freedom. They're far too independent for that, so they need a job that gives them room to breathe. If they don't have this, they're likely to cause havoc by staging lots of rows with their boss or finding other ways to show their displeasure.

Something else that makes an Arien see red is having to account for their every action or carry out someone's instructions to the letter without any opportunity to introduce their own ideas. If they're stuck in a job like this they'll quickly become bored and frustrated, in which case they need to develop some interesting hobbies into which they can channel all their creative energies.

The idea of being self-employed appeals to Ariens, who usually have a low opinion of their bosses and probably have one eye on their job. Their competitive nature makes them natural freelancers. They're great at coming up with new ideas but will struggle to keep up the momentum the moment they hit a boring patch. Most Ariens find it hard to cope with donkey work, especially if it persists for a long time.

Jobs connected with engineering, mechanics, the armed

services and sport all appeal to Ariens. If they want to get to the top of their particular tree they're quite capable of doing so, thanks to their competitive streak. They love coming first! They're also excellent at dreaming up ideas, although they're not so hot at following them through – they're far happier if someone else does that for them!

Money

An Arien can't live without money! They love spending it, so it may not be around for long. After all, an Arien can easily get carried away and part with far more money than they intended – often despite their best intentions to the contrary. They can't explain it – it just happens! Even a trip to the corner shop can result in the Arien struggling home weighed down by carrier bags. They're suckers for impulse buys.

Ariens also really enjoy spending money on anything connected with transport, such as sports cars, expensive motorbikes or the latest mountain bike, especially if they buy something fast and slightly dangerous.

Something else that can drain an Arien's pockets is their generosity. They can't bear the thought of stinginess, so would rather end up broke than accused of not paying their way. As a result they may overcompensate and buy loved ones all sorts of treats that they can't really afford, simply because they don't want to appear mean. High days and holidays find Ariens at their most vulnerable financially. Many of them like to leave the present-buying until the last minute, when they will dash around the shops in a panic, looking for the perfect gift. They usually end up spending far more money than they intended, simply because they know they can't go home empty-handed.

Red is the Aries colour and unfortunately their bank balance often reflects this. They aren't interested in saving money for the sake of it – if an Aries has some money in their pocket it will give them far more pleasure to spend it than to tuck it away for a rainy day. They want to live for today, not tomorrow!

Health

Ariens need to keep on the move. They are blessed with lots of vitality and energy, both of which require plenty of positive outlets. If an Arien can't get all this energy out of their system they soon start to feel restless, edgy and irritable. That's when the fur can start to fly! Ideally, they should join their local gym or play plenty of sports. Their naturally competitive spirit means they're always determined to come first when playing against other people, and they can be demons on the squash court. Agree to play against an Arien at your peril, unless you've already observed them on the quiet and know you can beat them.

Something that Ariens really aren't happy about is putting on weight when life becomes too sedentary and boring. An Arien's natural shape is lean and muscular, so they hate the thought of gaining extra pounds. However, very often this happens as a result of their love of food and drink. It's important for them to take plenty of exercise throughout their lives in order to stay in peak condition and to burn off those calories.

Each sign rules a particular area of the body and Aries rules the head. As a result, members of this sign are especially susceptible to bumps on the head, and they may even have a couple of facial scars as permanent reminders of previous escapades. Headaches could be a problem, especially if the Arien spends a lot of time cooped up indoors – being active in the fresh air helps to blow away the cobwebs and keeps them feeling fit. Drinking plenty of water will also help to keep those headaches at bay and combat potential kidney problems, which are linked to Libra, the opposite sign to Aries.

The World of Aries

Cities	Athens, Birmingham, Florence, Naples, Verona
Countries	Denmark, England, Germany
Colour	Red
Number	One
Day of the week	Tuesday
Gemstone	Diamond
Crystal	Carnelian
Animal	Ram
Foods	Chilli, onion, pepper, radish
Plants	Holly, nettle, poppy, thistle
Tarot card	The Emperor

Compatibility

Aries with Aries

This can be too much of a good thing! When two Ariens get together there is always a lot of friendly (or not so friendly) rivalry. They are always in competition with one another, even if it's tacit. They enjoy one another's company but can see vivid faults in the other that they are blind to in themselves.

Aries with Taurus

This is an awkward pairing. Aries and Taurus don't understand one another. The Arien likes to do things fast while the Taurean prefers to take their time. Even so, the Arien has much to teach the Taurean about being spontaneous, and the Taurean can encourage the Arien to look before they leap. But they must be patient with each other.

Aries with Gemini

Ariens and Geminis are on the same wavelength. They thoroughly enjoy each other's company because they share an enthusiasm for life and the desire to experience as much of it as possible. They're great friends, whatever their relationship. Sexually, however, the Arien may be too passionate and ardent for the Gemini's liking.

Aries with Cancer

Sparks can fly with this couple because their needs are so different. The Arien is loyal but needs plenty of time to follow their own interests, and the Cancerian needs to feel they're loved and cherished 24 hours a day. Stalemate! They're better as friends than lovers, when they'll run the risk of hurting each other without realizing it.

Aries with Leo

A good time is had by all when an Arien pairs up with a Leo. They both enjoy living it up, so it can be an expensive relationship. It's also a dramatic one, because both signs are hot-blooded and impetuous. They have a good time sexually, and all is well provided the Arien doesn't have a roving eye. The Leo won't stand for that!

Aries with Virgo

Plenty of tolerance is needed on both sides because they see life so differently. The Arien likes to do things on the spur of the moment but this worries the Virgo who prefers to plan in advance. The Arien can also be too messy and untidy for the neat Virgo to tolerate for long. They need to hit it off in the bedroom for this relationship to last.

Aries with Libra

These two have plenty to learn from one another. The diplomatic Libran, who instinctively puts others first, will learn to ask for what they want, while the self-centred Arien will learn to appreciate other people's needs. Even so, plenty of give and take is needed, preferably not with the Libran doing all the giving and the Arien all the taking.

Aries with Scorpio

Here are two people who share a passion for life. They have enough in common to keep them interested in one another, but their very different sexual needs may drive them apart. The Arien's easy-come-easy-go approach to romance will make the intense Scorpio suspect that they're just another notch on the bedpost.

Aries with Sagittarius

This relationship is expensive but good fun! They enjoy

leading each other astray, going to glitzy restaurants and doing plenty of globe-trotting. However, it will all fall apart very quickly if they don't laugh at each other's jokes! They get on very well sexually, provided everything stays light-hearted and easygoing.

Aries with Capricorn

It's a surprising combination but it works, provided they share the same ambitions. Both signs have a healthy respect for the good things in life and they'll work hard to get them. They also get on very well in the bedroom, because the Arien can encourage the Capricorn to forget their inhibitions and reveal their earthy side.

Aries with Aquarius

Friendship binds these two together. They're terrific mates, no matter what their relationship. Emotionally, however, they can hit problems if the Arien is very hot-blooded and passionate but the Aquarian is rather cool and detached. This will hurt the Arien and make them wonder what they're doing wrong.

Aries with Pisces

An Arien and a Piscean will struggle to maintain a sexual relationship for long. The Arien is too lusty and passionate for the sensitive Piscean, who will retreat emotionally, much to the Arien's bewilderment and hurt. However, they can be good friends, with the Arien encouraging the Piscean to take a few risks every now and then.

TAURUS

21 April – 21 May

The Taurus Personality

People know they can trust Taureans. They know Taureans are reliable, faithful, practical and definitely people to turn to in a crisis. After all that, it should come as no surprise that Taureans belong to the Earth element of the zodiac, making them responsible, steady and trustworthy. Taureans are people who can be counted on.

Taurus is one of the Fixed signs of the zodiac, which means that although Taureans are steadfast, they are also very resistant to the idea of change. It makes them feel nervous and as if everything is going to collapse around their ears. A Taurean always takes a long time to get used to any major alterations in their life, and they can feel dislocated by the resulting change for much longer than the people around them. As a result, a Taurean tends to slip into routines that quickly become ruts, because they'd rather know what each day is going to bring (even if it is boring or tediously predictable) than risk getting upset when their regular schedule is disturbed.

Some astrology books describe this sign as slow, but it would be fairer to say that Taureans take life at a measured pace. A Taurean can dash around when it suits them but a typical Taurean prefers to do things in their own time and in their own way – and will simply turn a deaf ear to anyone who tries to persuade them otherwise. In their favour, they have tremendous determination and willpower, but this can turn into a stubborn streak, with the Taurean digging in their heels and refusing to budge. Nothing will change their mind; people can go blue in the face trying to talk them round but they simply won't listen.

Being able to feed and clothe themselves is essential for any self-respecting Taurean. Taureans need their sense of self-worth and progress through life to be reflected in their possessions. This means Taureans can accumulate a lot of belongings because, subconsciously, they see these as status symbols. They then become hemmed in by their possessions because they start to rule their lives – Taureans can't run the risk of losing all these objects that mean so much to them. As a result, they can't break out in new directions even if they want to because they're scared of what they might lose in the process. Eventually, this can feel like a straitjacket, but it may be too scary to do anything about it.

Of all the members of the zodiac, a Taurean is the one least likely to lose their temper over trifles. The Taurean will grit their teeth and give people the benefit of the doubt again and again and again, until things go too far and they blow their top. This can be a frightening experience for everyone because a Taurean really knows how to let rip! It's a case of light the blue touchpaper and stand well back. What's more, a Taurean can smoulder for a long time after the initial row has blown over and everyone else has forgotten all about it.

Love

Family means the world to a Taurean, who will devote a lot of time to their nearest and dearest. Taureans feel comfortable around these people because they've known them for such a long time and don't have to make much of an effort with them. Taureans enjoy keeping up long-standing family traditions, especially at festive times of the year. They also like knowing that they don't have to do anything special to impress anyone!

Taureans are loyal, loving and steadfast. This endears them to anyone who likes to know that their affection won't be tossed away after the first, fine rapture has waned. A Taurean makes a devoted friend and they usually have a select circle of very close chums that they've known for a long time rather than a wide range of acquaintances. It takes a Taurean quite some time to get to know people properly, and others have to earn a Taurean's trust, but once they've done that the Taurean becomes the sort of pal who will stand by them through thick and thin. You can depend on a Taurean in a crisis.

Even though Taureans are very loving and affectionate, unfortunately this can sometimes turn into a tendency to be possessive. A Taurean can act this way towards friends and family as well as their partner, making it plain that they consider them to be their property. Sometimes a Taurean is so possessive that they hate to let their partner out of their sight and may object when other people lay claims on their time. Sadly, this is usually self-defeating because the person concerned won't enjoy being treated as if they are owned, and as if they're out on loan whenever they're away from the Taurean. If this possessiveness really starts to take root, the partner may run very fast in the opposite direction. Sadly, this may make the Taurean even more determined to cling on to the next person that they fall in love with. If a Taurean could only learn to let go, and understand that the best way to keep someone's love is to give them their freedom, they would be much happier. And so would the people involved with them.

Career

Some signs don't like the thought of hard work but the Taurean doesn't mind it one bit. In fact, they're a good, solid, reliable member of any team. You can rely on a Taurean to get the job done. They may not polish it off as quickly as some of their fellow Sun signs, but at least they'll do it properly and won't want to cut corners.

Self-employment isn't ideally suited to Taureans because they aren't happy with the thought of an irregular income and unpredictable working hours. However, they have plenty of discipline and motivation, so if a Taurean does decide to work for themselves they certainly won't fail through lack of trying. Their natural affinity with money means that any career connected with finance, such as banking, insurance, consultancy or investments, is right up their street.

Another career that suits members of this sign down to the ground is the beauty industry. This is perfect because a typical Taurean is a walking advert for beauty preparations (after all, this is one of the best-looking signs in the zodiac). They make great models, beauticians, masseurs, aromatherapists and perfumiers. Taureans also do well in professions connected with nature and the outdoors, such as farming, gardening and floristry. There are many Taureans in the music industry too, especially singers, because this sign is blessed with beautiful voices.

Money

Money and Taurus go together like bread and butter. A Taurean understands money and respects it for what it can buy them. This can be summed up in one word – security. They will have sleepless nights if they think they're going broke or they can't afford the roof over their head. A Taurean also needs to know there's enough money in the bank for a rainy day.

Their practical nature stands them in excellent stead when it comes to money matters because they always do their best to keep their finances up-to-date and in good order. Savings schemes appeal to the typical Taurean, who probably started to fill their piggy bank with coins as soon as they learned that two and two make four.

One of the first things Taureans like to do when they've got some money is to buy a home of their own. It makes them feel safe to know they have a permanent home that's a good investment and that they aren't giving their hard-earned cash to a landlord. Instead, they know they've got a nest-egg for the future, and are creating a comfortable home at the same time. This will make them doubly happy!

It's important for every Taurean to make adequate financial provision for the future, such as by investing in a solid pension and salting away any spare cash into reliable savings accounts. It's another way for them to bolster their physical and material security. But this doesn't mean that most Taureans are miserly or tight-fisted – on the contrary, they can be the soul of generosity and enjoy sharing what they've got with their loved ones. Taureans also like treating themselves to luxuries, especially if these will pamper them or help them to relax.

Health

Each sign rules a particular part of the body, and Taurus rules the throat. So every Taurean needs to look after their throat and neck because it may be their weak spot. When they feel run down they can easily develop a sore throat or a stiff neck. They might also go quite hoarse, or possibly lose their voice altogether, in times of great emotion or stress.

The other big Taurean bugbear is weight. Taureans enjoy taking life easy, and they also happen to enjoy a life-long love affair with food, and the results are all too easy to imagine – and to see. Taureans put on weight quickly but find it difficult to lose it again, thanks to their slow metabolism. It's important for them to get plenty of fresh air and to combat what could be a sedentary job with lots of exercise in their spare time. Something energetic like aerobics may not appeal, but they'll enjoy dancing or taking brisk walks in the countryside.

Being in the great outdoors is essential to a Taurean's well-being and happiness. This sign has a great love of nature and the countryside, so any Taurean who lives in a high-rise flat, miles from the nearest blade of grass, will soon start to feel that something's wrong. They need to reconnect with nature, even if that means growing pot plants in their home or tending a windowbox full of flowers or herbs.

Gardening is a great way for Taureans to unwind, because it literally helps to ground them. They also benefit from being able to walk barefoot through grass because it brings them into contact with the earth, which they find a very sensual experience.

The World of Taurus

Cities	Dublin, Leipzig, Lucerne, Mantua, Vatican City
Countries	Eire, Iran, Russia, Switzerland, Zambia
Colour	Green
Number	Six
Day of the week	Friday
Gemstone	Emerald
Crystal	Malachite
Animal	Bull
Foods	Apple, asparagus, wheat
Plants	Daisy, dandelion, violet
Tarot card	The Hierophant

Compatibility

Taurus with Aries

A Taurean struggles to work out what makes an Arien tick. They like to adopt a practical approach to life whereas the Arien wants to take everything at a rush. They can also feel short-changed emotionally, because the sort of smouldering passion they enjoy can make an Arien feel uncomfortable and trapped.

Taurus with Taurus

Although this couple instinctively understand one another, that isn't always a good thing. They feel so safe with each other that they can easily slip into a comfortable rut that excludes the rest of the world. The obstinacy that they share can also mean there's no room for manoeuvre whenever they fall out with each other.

Taurus with Gemini

It's difficult to make this pairing work, especially emotionally. The Taurean is too passionate and earthy for the light-hearted Gemini, who feels buried under an avalanche of emotioan. The Taurean will feel hurt if the Gemini devotes too much time to their independent social life. They're much happier as friends than lovers.

Taurus with Cancer

This is a pairing made in heaven! Both signs love their home and family, and they share a strong need for emotional and material security. They'll revel in nest-building and will devote many happy hours to cooking each other delicious but nourishing meals. Their sex life also keeps them smiling because they have the same needs.

Taurus with Leo

The Taurean appreciates the Leo brand of loving, and the Leo adores being with someone so faithful. The main problem arises when they have arguments. The Leo wants to be the boss and dictate terms, but the Taurean will stand their ground and refuse to budge an inch. They must both learn to go with the flow.

Taurus with Virgo

This couple understand one another on many levels. The Taurean enjoys the Virgo's practical nature but won't appreciate being nagged about their dietary habits. The Taurean also likes peace and quiet, so may have problems if the Virgo is very chatty. Emotionally, the Taurean will teach the Virgo to be more open.

Taurus with Libra

Both these people appreciate the finer things in life. They also share a need for their relationships to be harmonious and easygoing. However, the dogmatic Taurean may lose patience if the Libran likes to sit on the fence and rarely makes concrete decisions. Food and drink play a large part in their relationship!

Taurus with Scorpio

There's plenty of passion when these two get together. They'll raise the temperature in the bedroom by several degrees, enjoying a powerful sexual and emotional rapport. They feel safe with one another because they're both faithful and loyal. The placid Taurean will help the Scorpio to tone down their intense approach to life.

Taurus with Sagittarius

It's hard for these two to stay together for long because

they're poles apart. The Taurean is an instinctive home-lover while the Sagittarian is a born traveller. Possessiveness is bound to come between them, with the Taurean wanting – but failing – to hold on to the Sagittarian and to temper their need for independence.

Taurus with Capricorn

Both signs are too modest and conservative to admit it, but this is a very earthy and passionate combination. They know where they stand with each other and that they share the same down-to-earth approach to life. They also have a tacit agreement that the Taurean looks after the home and the Capricorn earns the money.

Taurus with Aquarius

This couple can't fathom one another. The Taurean enjoys tradition and is shocked when the Aquarian dismisses this as sentimental twaddle. The loving Taurean is also easily hurt by the Aquarian's need to maintain some emotional distance. They feel threatened by the Aquarian's love of independence and wonder what it means.

Taurus with Pisces

This duo enjoy one another's company and are good friends. The Taurean feels protective towards the sensitive Piscean and enjoys taking care of them. They can also encourage the Piscean to be more practical and organized. All is well provided the straightforward Taurean understands that their Piscean is a complicated being.

GEMINI

22 May – 21 June

Gemini

The Gemini Personality

This is one of the most lively and vibrant signs of the zodiac. Geminis are mercurial, bright and terrific company. Even better, they don't seem to age, and even when they're older than they care to remember they will still look years younger than they really are. Their attitude to life will also be a lot more youthful than their contemporaries. Geminis love keeping up with the latest trends and their insatiable curiosity makes them as interested in knowing what their best friend is doing as in what's happening on the other side of the world.

The growth of the Internet and the entire technological revolution is a real gift to Geminis because it has opened up whole new areas of communication. Not only can Geminis continue to enjoy reading books, magazines and newspapers, they can now chat to complete strangers through the ether and order their groceries through the television. And as for mobile phones . . . Well, chatterboxes like Geminis are in heaven!

It's certainly important for Geminis to keep in touch with

people, and if they are on the Internet they probably email friends and family in the four corners of the globe. But a Gemini is just as happy chatting to their next-door neighbour or getting together with friends. And if a Gemini is in the right mood they will gladly strike up a conversation with the person standing behind them in the supermarket queue or sitting next to them on the bus. Is this a polite way of saying that Geminis love gossiping? Well, yes, actually. There's nothing they like better than being first with the news – 'Remember, you heard it here first,' they'll say as they impart the latest snippet of information.

It's all thanks to their planetary ruler, Mercury. He rules communications and therefore makes Geminis very eloquent. The typical Gemini is a born communicator and finds it easy to express their ideas. Mercury is a liquid metal and Geminis also like to keep things fluid. In fact, Geminis can be really restless at times, unable to settle down to anything for long. As a result, they have a low boredom threshold and can find it difficult to concentrate on one thing for very long unless they're completely enraptured by it. If they aren't careful, this can lead to a superficial approach, with lots of projects left unfinished.

Versatility is a Gemini's middle name and they can

certainly tackle most things. A typical Gemini is also very adaptable, although sometimes this turns into moodiness and inconsistency. Geminis believe that they operate on a steady, even keel but the people in their life might not agree. Yes, a Gemini's emotions dip up and down dramatically. Yes, there are days when a Gemini doesn't want to talk to a soul and other days when they have to be physically prised off the phone. A Gemini might think that's just the way they operate, but others call it moodiness. It can also be hard to keep track of a Gemini's opinions because they tend to change them as often as they change the colour of their hair. Some people are wedded to their ideas through thick and thin; a Gemini fluctuates according to the circumstances and time of day. It's all part of what makes a Gemini such an interesting person to have around.

Love

The sign of Gemini belongs to the Air element, so Geminis are happiest when dealing with ideas. Emotions make them feel uncomfortable and it can be hard for them to express their feelings. A Gemini has just as many feelings as anyone else, of course, but they aren't very happy when dealing with them. In fact, emotions can make a Gemini embarrassed, tongue-tied and feel as though they've got two left feet. They can also feel swamped by a partner who is very emotional. Because a Gemini has such a gift for words they can describe their emotions in an intellectual way but it is another story when it comes to experiencing and living their feelings. Anyone who wears their heart on their sleeve makes a Gemini wince and want to rush off in the opposite direction.

There are problems when a Gemini is in a relationship with someone who's very clingy or possessive, because this is almost guaranteed to make them do a rapid disappearing act. Unfortunately, sometimes the partner has good reason to want to keep tabs on their Gemini – some members of this sign are not exactly noted for their fidelity. Especially when young, they can enjoy playing partners off against each other or getting involved in some complex two-timing.

Even so, a Gemini's popularity rating is usually sky-high. People adore their sunny nature, their ready laugh and their fascinating conversation. A typical Gemini knows a little about an awful lot. When looking for friends and lovers, a Gemini seeks out people who are on the same intellectual wavelength as themselves and who make them think. No matter how devastatingly attractive someone is, a Gemini won't stay with them for long if they're boring, not very bright or don't have a sense of humour. The Gemini will soon have other fish to fry.

Career

Communicating with others is second nature to Geminis, so it's wise for them to find a career in which this is an essential ingredient. Most Geminis will find it a struggle to become a Trappist monk or to do anything else that involves long periods of silence. They simply aren't cut out for that quiet a life!

Geminis find it easy to get on well with their colleagues and clients – everyone warms to the Gemini's breezy personality and the Gemini enjoys getting to know their workmates as people in their own right, not simply as colleagues. This natural ability to communicate makes a Gemini an ideal candidate for any job in the media, communications industry, advertising or sales. A Gemini also needs a job that keeps them busy, with plenty of variation in their daily schedule and, ideally, the chance to go travelling.

Because a Gemini finds it easy to do at least two things at once, or to tackle several projects at one time and to switch between them according to their mood, self-employment may also suit them. However, they must cultivate the mental discipline to carry on working on those days when they'd rather stay in bed.

Whatever their job happens to be, you can expect a Gemini to be completely clued up about the latest office gossip. They're the one to ask if you want to know what's going on!

Money

Money is like a conjuring trick for a Gemini. Now you see it, now you don't. A Gemini can spend their cash as soon as they get it! Although they appreciate the theory of saving money, it rarely happens in practice because there are too many tempting items for them to buy.

One area in which Geminis excel is in wheeling and dealing. These people have such a good sales pitch that they could sell fish to penguins. They're excellent at negotiating good deals and bargains.

A big expense for many Geminis is keeping in touch with the rest of the world. Many run up massive phone bills because they love chatting and keeping up with the gossip.

They also enjoy spending money on the latest computer equipment because they like to keep abreast of technology. If they can afford it, they'll buy themselves all sorts of neat gadgets, such as computer notebooks and the very latest mobile phones.

Geminis like to tell themselves that finance doesn't mean much to them and that there are more important things in life than having a healthy bank balance or a portfolio of shares, yet they certainly enjoy the things that money can buy. Finance in itself might bore the typical Gemini to tears, but if they turn it into an intellectual game they can become absolutely fascinated. For instance, they will enjoy reading the business pages of newspapers in the same way they read a gossip column – 'Hey, did you see that Knitted Socks Incorporated has just paid $6 billion for Global Mouthwash? I wonder if they'll buy Earplugs United next?' – although the latest movements in their bank account might be a complete mystery to them.

They also enjoy impulse shopping, which can have a drastic effect on their bank balance. Overdrawn? Am I really? How on earth did that happen? It couldn't have anything to do with that pile of clothes I just bought, could it?

Health

A Gemini may give the impression of being game for anything and ready to stay up all night, but underneath it all they have a very sensitive nervous system. A Gemini is like a clock that looks sturdy and reliable but which goes wrong whenever the mechanism gets out of balance. And that is quite often. One of the easiest ways for a Gemini's system to go wrong is if they are bored. If they go through a period when their life becomes mundane and unexciting, it can make them feel quite ill. When this happens the Gemini needs to find positive outlets for their nervous energy, such as tennis, which is the perfect Gemini sport. A Gemini certainly likes it when life is busy and lively, and much prefers this to slack times, although too many late nights will soon catch up with them. So will the typical Gemini diet of too much coffee and cigarettes and not enough solid food.

The average Gemini is no stranger to bouts of insomnia. Ideally, they should be active during the day so they crawl into bed and can't wait to fall asleep. Otherwise, their busy brain will start churning away the moment their head hits the pillow, and it can keep them awake for hours.

Most signs fight the battle of the bulge, but many Geminis suffer from the opposite problem and find it difficult to gain weight. It's a problem that makes other signs go green with envy!

Gemini rules the arms, hands and chest, so these are the most vulnerable areas of a Gemini's body. Typical Geminis gesticulate all the time while talking – even on the phone – so it's hardly surprising that occasionally these limbs make contact with something hard and the result is a bruise, strain or even a fracture.

The World of Gemini

Cities	Cardiff, London, Melbourne, San Francisco
Countries	Barbados, Belgium, Sardinia, Wales
Colour	Yellow
Number	Five
Day of the week	Wednesday
Gemstone	Garnet
Crystal	Agate
Animal	Monkey
Foods	Carrot, nuts
Plants	Buttercup, lavender, lily of the valley
Tarot card	The Magician

Compatibility

Gemini with Aries

They really enjoy one another's company and share an insatiable curiosity about the world. This is the sort of couple that always get each other into scrapes that they laugh their way out of. Emotionally, the ardent and fiery

Arien can be hurt by the easygoing Gemini, who sometimes struggles to show their feelings.

Gemini with Taurus

What do these people see in each other? They're much better friends than lovers because they have such different emotional needs. Also, the quick-witted Gemini soon loses their patience with the pragmatic Taurean. The Gemini's ability to see at least two sides in an argument flummoxes the straightforward Taurean.

Gemini with Gemini

When one Gemini pairs up with another, they're relieved to find someone who truly understands them. They'll soon develop lots of in-jokes and will delight in trading puns and wisecracks. It will help if they are comfortable with showing their feelings, otherwise the relationship may become rather unemotional.

Gemini with Cancer

This is a super combination for business or friendship, but

it isn't so hot for romance because these people are so different. At first, the Gemini enjoys the novelty value of being cherished by their Cancerian, but after a while they may start to feel suffocated and trapped. They're convinced there's more to life than home cooking.

Gemini with Leo

This fun-loving pair are made for each other. They share a terrific sense of humour and love teasing one another. The Gemini will gently bring the Leo down to earth when they get too full of themselves. The Gemini also revels in being the focus of the Leo's attention, although they may sometimes feel they can have too much of a good thing.

Gemini with Virgo

Put together two of the great communicators of the zodiac and what do you get? A lot of talk! This couple can chat right round the clock, always finding something new to discuss. However, such an emphasis on brainpower can hold them back emotionally, because neither of them is comfortable when talking about their feelings.

Gemini with Libra

This is one of the great combinations and both signs get a lot out of the relationship. They both look for clever partners so are secretly flattered that the other one obviously rates them intellectually. They're good friends, lovers or business partners. If anyone can encourage a Gemini to express their softer and more romantic side, it's a Libran.

Gemini with Scorpio

This couple has virtually nothing in common yet they make surprisingly good friends. Both of them are naturally curious and they're intrigued to know what makes the other one tick. But it's a different story in a sexual relationship, because the Gemini finds the Scorpio far too hot, heavy and passionate for comfort.

Gemini with Sagittarius

These people instinctively understand and complement one another on many levels. They share a love of mental and physical exploration, so always have something to talk about. They both have passing enthusiasms, although the Gemini may learn to go into things in more depth after spending time with the Sagittarian.

Gemini with Capricorn

It's the odd couple! All is well if the Capricorn has a dry sense of humour, but the Gemini will soon get fed up if they're with the sort of Capricorn who is morose and pessimistic. Even so, the Gemini can teach the Capricorn to lighten up, and can learn in return to take life a little more seriously. Sexually, it's either great or ghastly.

Gemini with Aquarius

Neither sign tolerates fools, so both individuals have to keep their brains up to the mark if they want the relationship to last. They enjoy getting involved in long discussions about whatever pops into their minds. Even if their relationship starts romantically, they will eventually become best friends, sometimes at the expense of their sex life.

Gemini with Pisces

They're good friends, although they occasionally have misunderstandings that upset the Piscean. However, they struggle to maintain a happy emotional relationship because there is so much scope for misunderstanding. The Gemini's glib remarks and sometimes cool emotions can quickly make the Piscean retreat in bewilderment.

CANCER

22 June – 23 July

Cancer

The Cancer Personality

One of the first things people notice about Cancerians is their kindness. Cancerians belong to one of the most caring and sensitive signs in the zodiac, and this makes them very popular with anyone who likes to feel cherished. It's partly thanks to the Moon, which rules the sign of Cancer, and partly to the fact that Cancerians belong to the Water element. Put those two things together and you get someone who is considerate, affectionate and highly emotional.

The typical Cancerian loves being at home, not only because it's cosy and comfortable but because it's where they feel safest. A Cancerian may not even realize it, but they've probably filled their home with all sorts of precious mementoes and keepsakes that remind them of the past and of their loved ones. They may also have cupboards and drawers filled with all sorts of things that they no longer use but can't bear to throw away. For instance, a Cancerian might keep a sweater even though it's full of holes, simply because they wore it on their first date with their partner and it's now a part of their life.

Cancer

Cancer is the sign of the crab, and sure enough Cancerians tend to lead their lives in very crab-like ways. For instance, they often approach situations from an angle rather than directly. They have a tendency to manipulate people into doing what they want instead of making outright requests. They also tend to retreat into their shell whenever the going gets tough or they think they aren't appreciated. Cancerians are very good at going into huffs and sulks when things don't go their way. They may not even realize that they're doing it, although everyone else knows what's going on!

Because this is a Water sign, Cancerians often soak up the atmosphere around them like a sponge. They are also very sensitive to other people's moods so will quickly take on the feelings of the person they're talking to. Some of them may even be psychic or have pronounced ESP abilities.

Family life means everything to members of this sign. If a Cancerian doesn't get on well with their own kith and kin, or if they live very far away from them, they will compensate by creating a close-knit group of special friends. The Cancerian thinks of these people as their ready-made family and are really proud of their achievements. And you can bet that these people consider themselves very lucky to be looked after by a Cancerian!

Love

Even though a Cancerian is highly emotional, there is a very shrewd side to them. It makes them a great judge of character. However, their emotions often get in the way of their judgement of people, making them either completely for or against them. Even if a Cancerian is aware of what's going on it can be almost impossible for them to divorce themselves from their feelings.

The people in a Cancerian's life think of them as very affectionate, loving and demonstrative. That's thanks to their strong maternal instinct, which operates whether they're a man or a woman. Unfortunately, however, this doting affection can sometimes become too stifling for anyone who's very independent, because they start to feel smothered. If the Cancerian is honest, they'll admit that they can occasionally cling to people and are reluctant to let them out of their sight. This isn't because they want to control them, simply because they find it comforting being around their loved ones.

A Cancerian can also struggle to allow a relationship to come to the end of its natural life. They will pretend that nothing is wrong and try to keep the partnership going for as long as possible, even if it's making them unhappy. They find it very hard to say goodbye.

A Cancerian is in clover when things are going well in a relationship, but they can become awfully moody and tense when they suspect that something's gone wrong. The bottom immediately falls out of their world. A Cancerian can become so defensive that they'll deliberately spark off a row, just so they can fire the first shot before the other person gets the chance to hurt them. If they can learn to relax more, and not take things so seriously, their relationships will run much more smoothly and there will be fewer tears and less heartache.

Career

A typical Cancerian has a marvellous business brain, making them a natural candidate for a successful career. Cancerians know what they want from life and, what's more, they know how to get it. A Cancerian is certainly not afraid of hard work, provided they're paid a decent wage and don't feel they are being exploited. Any job that involves looking after other people is ideal for them, especially if they work in one of the caring professions or a service industry. Children mean a lot to a Cancerian, so they might enjoy being a nanny, nurse or nursery teacher. Something else that would appeal is working in the antiques trade, or as a silversmith.

The sign of Cancer has a strong affinity with history, so a Cancerian might enjoy being a historian, archivist or an archaeologist. They also have a fascination with photography, so could combine two enthusiasms by working in a photographic archive.

If a Cancerian fancies a profession that comes completely naturally to them, catering might well be a good one. Many Cancerians are fantastic cooks, with an inbuilt understanding of what other people like to eat. A Cancerian might enjoy running their own bakery or restaurant, especially if they have a group of much-loved regular clients rather than a lot of anonymous passing trade. They will do their utmost to cater to their every need. It's another way to look after people.

Another possible string to a Cancerian's bow is comedy. Cancer is one of the signs that rule comedy because it places such a strong importance on familiar things, and we often laugh at jokes because their subject matter strikes a chord with us.

A Cancerian is much happier working with other people than on their own, when they will soon become lonely and depressed. However, when working with other people they should try hard not to absorb the atmosphere around them when things get tense, because this will make them feel ill. They need to cultivate a sense of detachment and self-preservation.

Money

Financially, Cancerians have got it taped! It may be difficult for them to keep control of their emotions but it's a very different story when it comes to their finances. Cancerians always have the upper hand financially, but only because they value the things that money can buy and the happiness it can bring to their loved ones. For example, one of a Cancerian's biggest priorities in life is to live in a comfortable home, preferably owned rather than rented. A Cancerian doesn't mind working hard to achieve this because it's important for them to return home to their own little nest every day. And they are so clued up financially that they know it is a waste of money to pay rent when they could be spending the cash on their own mortgage.

Something that a Cancerian always enjoys is spending money on their loved ones. They adore buying them little treats and big gifts and, as the recipient is always thrilled to get them, everyone's happy. A typical Cancerian isn't a flashy spender because they respect money too much to fritter it away. Instead, they choose very carefully and buy well-made items that are built to last.

Saving comes naturally to a Cancerian, who enjoys the satisfaction of seeing a nest-egg gradually grow in size over the years. They aren't interested in get-rich-quick schemes because they're well aware of the risks involved, so they prefer slow and steady ways of increasing their capital. These may not be very exciting but at least the Cancerian knows they're safe. If a Cancerian is looking for interesting ways to invest their money, they might be instinctively drawn to antiques and items made from silver. That's because this is the metal ruled by Cancer, and because Cancerians have a strong affinity with things from the past.

Health

Because their feelings are so central to a Cancerian's existence, every area of their life is bound to have an emotional impact on them. This can have a huge effect on their health, especially when they are upset about something.

Cancer

The results are usually stomach problems and digestive upsets, as well as an unpleasant, jittery feeling that doesn't want to go away. The best way to combat such ailments is for the Cancerian to learn to relax more and not to take life so seriously, but that's a lot easier said than done because every Cancerian is a born worrier. And they don't only worry about themselves. They can fret about their loved ones, their pets, the weather – you name it. If worrying were an Olympic sport, Cancerians would have shelves full of trophies!

One excellent way for them to relax is to spend time near water. Listening to the waves crashing on a beach, sailing on a lake, going swimming or strolling along a riverbank are all good ways for them to unwind. Or they can always relax in a warm, scented bath!

Food is a great source of comfort to a Cancerian, especially when things are going wrong. They are particularly fond of the sort of food that's high in calories and fat, but unfortunately the effects of this are often more than obvious. As they say, a moment on the lips, a lifetime on the hips. Even so, cooking is a wonderful form of therapy for them and, as they are usually fantastic cooks, anyone they're cooking for will benefit as well.

As a Cancerian gets older they may find that there's a lot more of them than they'd like. They should make sure they get plenty of exercise to counter the effects of too many calories. This will also give them something else to think about besides all those worries.

The World of Cancer

Cities	Amsterdam, Cadiz, New York, Tokyo
Countries	Africa, New Zealand, Scotland
Colours	Mother-of-pearl, pearly grey, silver
Number	Two
Day of the week	Monday
Gemstone	Pearl
Crystal	Onyx
Animal	Crab
Foods	Cucumber, lettuce, milk, shellfish
Plants	Gardenia, lily, waterlily
Tarot card	The Chariot

Compatibility

Cancer with Aries

It's tough for these two to understand each other. The Cancerian way to anyone's heart is through their stomach, and this works at first for the Arien who adores being the culinary centre of attention. But it palls after a while and the Cancerian needs to give their Arien plenty of room to breathe. Sexually, though, it's hot stuff.

Cancer with Taurus

It's a marriage made in heaven! Comfort, cosiness and emotional safety are top priorities for both signs so they've got it made when they get together. At last, the Cancerian has found someone who enjoys being looked after and who shares their love of home comforts. The only problem is that they can get stuck in a conservative rut.

Cancer with Gemini

This is a strange mixture, especially in an emotional relationship. The Cancerian admires the way the Gemini rushes around doing several things at once, but can't match their hectic pace for long. They enjoy taking care of the Gemini but need to back off every now and then, otherwise the Gemini can feel smothered.

Cancer with Cancer

When two homebodies pair up, it may take a miracle to get them out of their own front door for longer than a trip to the shops. They will devote a lot of time and love to making sure their home is as cosy and welcoming as possible. They both need to talk about their feelings if they want to avoid long sulks and nasty silences when things go wrong.

Cancer with Leo

Both signs place a big emphasis on the family, which immediately gives them a lot in common. They also enjoy looking after each other, ideally with the Leo wearing the trousers. Although they're both good at expressing their feelings, sometimes the Cancerian can retreat into sulks which will soon get the Leo roaring with anger.

Cancer with Virgo

It's hard to know what these two see in each other. The Cancerian is a natural hoarder but the Virgo sees this as a way of collecting dust. All those rib-sticking Cancerian meals can also go unappreciated by the health-conscious Virgo. Emotionally, the Cancerian can feel short-changed by their no-nonsense, sensible Virgo.

Cancer with Libra

Despite their many differences, this couple really appreciate each other. Neither of them likes conflict so they'll work hard to maintain a harmonious relationship. When problems arise, the Cancerian will sulk about them and the Libran will brush them under the carpet. They will both find it hard to say goodbye if the relationship ends.

Cancer with Scorpio

What a happy couple! They share the same intense emotional needs, although at times their private life can become as emotionally charged as a melodramatic opera. There may be scenes and massive rows, but they'll both enjoy making up afterwards. Sexually, they have a very erotic and sensual time together.

Cancer with Sagittarius

This is not a natural pairing because the Cancerian is a homemaker while the Sagittarian prefers to explore the world. Friendship between them is interesting because of their differences but any strong emotional contact will be fraught with difficulties. The Cancerian is easily hurt by the Sagittarian's blunt style of honesty.

Cancer with Capricorn

If there's one person a Cancerian feels safe with, it's a Capricorn. They know they'll be looked after and that this person will treat them with respect. In return, they'll provide a happy home for the Capricorn. However, they wear their heart on their sleeve and it is easily damaged by the buttoned-down Capricorn.

Cancer with Aquarius

What do these two see in each other? The Cancerian

doesn't know what to make of the wacky Aquarian, who may deliberately wind them up to see how they react. They will also be horrified when the Aquarian suggests breaking traditions or says they've seen too much of the Cancerian's family. This relationship is hard work.

Cancer with Pisces

Here are two people who understand one another. They'll enjoy taking care of each other and can happily share their feelings. However, they aren't so good at talking about any problems between them. A favourite pastime is watching tear-jerker films and indulging in orgies of weeping. They'll have a lovely time!

Leo

24 July – 23 August

The Leo Personality

This is the most regal sign of the zodiac. After all, lions are kings of the jungle and Leo is the sign of the lion. Every Leo worth their salt has an air of dignity and they behave accordingly. It's as if Leos know they're different from everyone else and don't want us to forget it. That's because Leos are ruled by the Sun which is, after all, the centre of our solar system and literally the light of our lives. We would die without the Sun and, on some level, Leos know that everyone else would wither up without them. Leos are life-enhancing!

If you're trying to spot a Leo, look at their hair first. Most Leos have luxuriant, thick manes, and always take a lot of trouble over them. Their hair is one of the first things you'll notice about them. If they can afford it, they will spend lots of money on all the best treatments and products.

Leo belongs to the Fire element, which makes members of this sign very exuberant and enthusiastic. They are also very warm and affectionate. In fact, everyone needs at least one Leo in their lives, simply for the many ego boosts they'll receive from their Leo friend. It's also good to know that, as Leos don't suffer fools gladly, you seem to have passed the acid test and been accepted into their inner circle.

With their royal connections, occasionally Leos can be snobby and far too full of themselves. Luckily, however, these are the exception that proves the rule. They are the grand, conceited people who give all the other Leos a bad name. Most Leos are quietly confident and don't feel the need to prove how great they are. All the same, it's very important for a Leo to feel they've made an impression on people, but this happens quite naturally – a Leo doesn't have to put on airs and graces to do it.

One area in which Leos excel is in organization. They're brilliant at making things happen, especially if that means whipping other people into shape. They simply have a natural air of authority that makes everyone else sit up and take notice.

Family matters are very dear to every Leo's heart. They place a lot of importance on keeping in touch with scattered members of the clan. They also like gathering their relatives around them every now and then. Like their namesake lions, they have a big interest in their children and will teach them to stand on their own two feet.

Leo is the sign of creativity, and any Leo who can't express their talents in one way or another will soon become frustrated and irritable. Of course, creativity comes in many forms, but key Leo activities include dancing, acting and painting. They also enjoy appreciating other people's artistic abilities, especially in the cinema and theatre. This is the sign of drama!

Love

Love and Leo go together. The sign of Leo rules the heart and Leos find it very easy to show affection to the people in their lives. In fact, the typical Leo has a huge heart and boundless supplies of love for everyone they care about. Once someone has captured a Leo's affections they'll always retain a place in the Leo's heart unless they hurt them so deeply that they can never forgive them. For a sign with such a dignified, stately reputation, a Leo is surprisingly vulnerable underneath that confident exterior and people often trample on their feelings without realizing it. The Leo's pride makes them reluctant to reveal that they've been hurt, although when things get really bad they'll make a big song and dance about it, roaring their objections and being full of righteous indignation.

Loyalty comes high on a Leo's list of emotional priorities – they are extremely faithful and expect their lover to behave in the same way. Because this is a Fire sign, it's second nature for a Leo to show their affection with plenty of hugs and kisses. Sex is also an important way for a Leo to demonstrate their expansive affections. If a Leo is denied these all-important outlets, perhaps because their partner is very undemonstrative or they're currently single, they will have to find other ways of expressing their emotions. Their friends can look forward to being cherished and made a big fuss of!

There's only one small snag in relationships, and that's the Leo's tendency to boss other people about. It's not that the Leo means to do it, more that they simply can't help themselves! If a Leo knows what someone should do for the best, they can't resist telling them. Half the time the Leo doesn't even realize they're doing this, so they need a partner who can stand up to them and possibly even tick them off every now and then. It's very important for the Leo to understand that they can't call the shots all the time. There has to be give and take, so the Leo can enjoy an equal partnership and not preside over a dictatorship.

Career

A Leo has tremendous potential and can turn their hand to virtually anything. A typical Leo adores stretching themselves by discovering fresh talents and skills, and they are also blessed with plenty of creative and artistic ability. It's a matter of pride for a Leo to know they're putting everything into their work, so they will feel let down and cheated if their job fails to live up to their expectations or they suspect they're wasting their time. They will also quickly become disillusioned if their colleagues aren't pulling their weight.

A Leo needs to be emotionally involved with their work, and anything less than that simply won't do. It will upset them if their efforts go unnoticed by their boss or colleagues. A Leo doesn't expect to be praised every five minutes but they certainly like to know they're appreciated.

Leos excel at anything involving organization – if a Leo can't make things happen, no one can. A Leo will derive enormous satisfaction from setting up systems and making sure that everyone does what's expected of them – any shirkers will soon be told to pull their socks up. Sometimes, however, the people who work with them will accuse them of being bossy and demanding. They can also be rather pompous at times, and may need to be gently taken down a peg or two. Usually, they'll soon see the funny side as their sense of humour takes over.

Leos need to take centre-stage in some way. It's a rare Leo who's content to work on the sidelines or to let someone else enjoy the limelight. That's why so many Leos work in the entertainment industry as actors, dancers, singers and designers. Leos also enjoy using their many creative and artistic talents in other ways, such as painting, fashion, sport and cooking.

Money

Leos need money because they have certain standards that they like to maintain. Only the best is good enough for a Leo! As a result, their finances may be permanently stretched to the limit. A Leo's idea of heaven is to go into the most expensive shop they can find and then buy up as many luxuries as possible. They like to have the best because they believe they deserve it. Besides, they can't see the point in buying anything second-rate if they don't have to. A Leo will ignore anything cheap and nasty, and will head straight for the best objects that money can buy. Quality not quantity is their motto, and if something is tacky or shoddy they'd rather go without, thank you very much. The Leo will quietly bide their time until they can buy the best model available.

Loved ones benefit from the innate Leo generosity because a Leo adores lavishing presents on them, just to let them know they care. It gives a Leo tremendous delight to spoil their favourite people, no matter how much it costs.

Of course, it goes without saying that a Leo needs a steady income in order to pay for all these gifts, as well as those treats for themselves. The Leo also needs to put some money away for the future, so they've got something to draw on if times are hard or they need cheering up. Despite being an enthusiastic Fire sign, a Leo likes to stick to traditional ways of saving money. If they're looking for an interesting investment they could be attracted to expensive jewellery or objects made of gold – that way, they can enjoy wearing their nest-egg.

Health

It won't come as a surprise to hear that a Leo's love of the good life can have a dramatic effect on their waistline. Unless a Leo takes a lot of exercise, it's easy for them to put on weight and very hard for them to shift it again. This is something that every self-respecting Leo loathes because they always like to look their very best. Although exercise is important for every sign it's essential for Leos, because without it they can become very sluggish and irritable. Of course, it helps to know that it will streamline their bodies as well and keep them looking wonderful.

Two areas of the body are ruled by Leo – the heart and the back. A Leo therefore needs to keep their heart healthy by avoiding too many fatty foods and making sure they keep fit. Emotionally they are big-hearted but they need to try to avoid making that a physical reality. They should look after their vulnerable back by investing in well-made chairs and a good-quality bed. It will also help if they can learn how to lift objects properly without damaging their delicate lumbar region.

If the thought of working out in a gym makes a Leo so exhausted that they want to lie down, they should try to combine taking exercise with something sociable. For instance, they could join a sports club that has an excellent restaurant or bar, or get together with a group of friends so they can have a good laugh while keeping fit. Dancing is perfect for a Leo, because it allows them to express their considerable creative talents and to keep fit at the same time. Swimming is also good for them because the water will support their body and prevent them harming their joints. They can also spend many happy hours in shops looking for the perfect swimsuit!

The World of Leo

Cities	Bristol, Chicago, Los Angeles, Rome
Countries	Italy (including Sicily), Romania
Colours	Gold, orange
Number	One
Day of the week	Sunday
Gemstone	Ruby
Crystal	Rose quartz
Animals	All members of the cat family
Foods	Honey, citrus fruits, olives, rice
Plants	Camomile, daffodil, marigold, sunflower
Tarot card	Strength

Compatibility

Leo with Aries

There's much excitement with this pairing. Both like to throw themselves into life and egg each other on to further exploits. The Leo's dignity can sometimes be shaken by the Arien tendency to blurt out their thoughts, but their sense of humour will see them through. Sexually, sparks can fly!

Leo with Taurus

Everything will go swimmingly with this couple until they fail to see eye to eye. When this happens, hell could freeze over before either of them is prepared to back down or say sorry. They need to find ways around this fixity. The Leo values loyalty and enjoys knowing that their Taurean will stand by them through thick and thin.

Leo with Gemini

This couple really know how to have fun. They instinctively like each other and get on well in both platonic and passionate relationships. The Leo enjoys the

Gemini's bubbly personality but can sometimes feel frustrated by their apparent inability to stop joking around and talk about their deepest feelings. They should encourage the Gemini to unwind.

Leo with Cancer

This pair have a lot going for them. They're both family-minded and so enjoy gathering their kith and kin around them. The Leo will greatly enjoy using their brilliant organizational skills on their sometimes chaotic Cancerian. The Leo will also excel at comforting the Cancerian when life gets them down, but won't want to mop up the tears too often.

Leo with Leo

The big question is which one of them will be boss? When two Leos get together, power struggles are bound to erupt sooner or later. Ideally, they should mark out different areas of territory so they both rule the roost at times. Emotionally and sexually, they're hot stuff. Financially, this could be a very expensive combination!

Leo with Virgo

This isn't the easiest combination in the world. The enthusiastic Leo will soon become irritated by the Virgo's pedantic need to nail down details, and frustrated by their reluctance to act on the spur of the moment. There may also be clashes over expenditure, with the Leo wanting to splash out while the Virgo prefers to count the pennies.

Leo with Libra

Here we have the two signs for whom love makes the world go round. They get on like a house on fire, although sometimes the Leo will be irritated by the Libran's inability to make up their mind. Romantically and sexually, however, they're in heaven. They're terrific friends, perfect lovers and good business partners.

Leo with Scorpio

This is a powerful combination, provided the Leo is prepared to be swept along by the Scorpio's intense attitude to life. There can be no half-measures with this relationship – the Scorpio simply won't allow it. This could be the greatest sexual passion the Leo has ever encountered but they'll balk at the Scorpio's tendency to be suspicious and jealous.

Leo with Sagittarius

These two spur each other on to all sorts of adventures. They're enthusiastic about life and enjoy spending money, so it could be an expensive pairing, especially when it comes to travel. The sky's the limit with these two! The Leo will enjoy the Sagittarian's sense of humour but may feel they aren't always treated with the respect they think they deserve.

Leo with Capricorn

Outward impressions are everything for these two. They share the need to cut a dash and command respect, so they'll work hard to create the image of the perfect couple. But it may be different behind the scenes, with the Leo sometimes feeling sidelined by the Capricorn's workaholic tendencies and their emotional reserve.

Leo with Aquarius

These people are fascinated by each other. They're very different yet they secretly admire one another for those very differences. They have plenty to talk about but the Leo can feel neglected emotionally if the Aquarian finds it hard to show their feelings or be physically demonstrative. Even if they break up, they'll stay friends.

Leo with Pisces

This is a strange pairing. Although both signs are very affectionate and loving, that's just about all they have in common. Is it enough to hold them together? Only if the Leo has the patience to weather all those Piscean storms of emotion and doesn't tear their hair out when their Piscean's life descends into total chaos yet again.

VIRGO

24 August – 23 September

Virgo

The Virgo Personality

It's tough being a Virgo. Some signs always get a good press but Virgo seems to attract a heap of criticism. Even when a Virgo tells you their Sun sign they'll often add apologetically that they know how boring they are. But is this fair?

For instance, Virgos are perfectionists. They like to do things properly and will be furious with themselves if they think they've turned in a second-rate job. Unfortunately, sometimes this means they can't leave something alone and will fiddle with it endlessly, trying to improve on what they've already done. They can also worry a lot about tiny details. When they wake up in the middle of the night, their first thought may be that they forgot to do something during the day. Then they can't get back to sleep for worrying about it.

But when you want something done, who do you turn to? The person who couldn't really care less whether they do the job properly, or the person who will stick at it until they're happy with the results? In other words, given the chance you'd choose a Virgo every time. We all would.

Virgo is the second sign of the Earth element, which

Virgo

means that a Virgo takes a very practical approach to life. This makes them wonderfully methodical, efficient and sensible, and also means that they're a tower of strength in a crisis. People rely on them but may also take them for granted.

The famous Virgo modesty means that any Virgo who's reading this will now have flaming red cheeks and be thinking 'Aw, shucks'. A Virgo's opinion of themselves is often much lower than everyone else's because they're so aware of what they see as their failings. These are the sorts of faults that everyone suffers from, but the Virgo will view them as major character flaws. Why can't they be tidier, neater, more organized … Needless to say, no one else would recognize the Virgo from their own character assessment.

Another very Virgoan characteristic is being critical. Virgos have very high standards and apply these rigorously. As a result, they can sound rather harsh and unsympathetic at times. Instead of heaping praise on someone's head in order to encourage them to greater things in future, a Virgo can sometimes be rather lukewarm in their enthusiasm or will unerringly pick on the one thing that the person didn't do properly. When you're on the receiving end of this sort of treatment, it may help to remind yourself that the Virgo is even tougher on themselves.

Virgos dislike drawing attention to themselves so they often prefer to blend into the woodwork than to stand out from the crowd. They may choose classic clothes in conservative colours rather than the latest fashion, and their wardrobe is often dominated by navy, black and grey. They like to look neat and well turned out, and will rarely look messy, even if they've been up all night.

Love

When it comes to relationships, a Virgo can struggle with their feelings. It is very hard for them to show their emotion, perhaps because this reveals the vulnerable side of their personality that they're always at pains to cover up. This can cause misunderstandings with loved ones, especially when a Virgo is under pressure. This is when their most unattractive trait comes to the surface – their ability to carp and criticize. There are times when a Virgo's standards are so high that no one can ever hope to live up to them, and they'll waste no time in telling everyone so. This sort of behaviour can definitely drive a wedge between a Virgo and their loved ones, because no one likes being continually assessed and found wanting. If this is a problem for a Virgo, they should be encouraged to relax more, to think before they speak and to let their natural kindness come to the fore. They should also ask themselves why it's so important for things to be done perfectly and whether the sky will fall in if they aren't.

Virgos are much more brainy than their fellow Earth signs, Taurus and Capricorn. They enjoy analysing situations and need a partner who will share their need to talk things through. This is not a sign that suffers fools gladly so they will soon lose patience with anyone who has fluff for brains or can only talk about events in their favourite soap opera.

Despite their modest and polite appearance, a Virgo can be pretty hot stuff in the bedroom. They enjoy casting aside that reserved demeanour! But they can become tongue-tied when it comes to saying how they feel. They can even find it difficult to be verbally demonstrative with friends, let alone lovers, so need someone who will encourage them to open up more.

Career

We all rely on Virgos. The world would fall apart in two days if it weren't for all the Virgos ensuring everything runs smoothly and efficiently. They're so practical and efficient that they excel at making sure offices, businesses and organizations are ticking over. Whenever a Virgo is ill or on holiday, things tend to grind to a halt because no one else knows what's going on or how things work. Virgos are brilliant at creating filing systems and other arrangements that make everything run like clockwork.

Speaking of clockwork, most Virgos are very good time-keepers. They don't like to be kept waiting by others and so they take pride in making sure they're on time as often as possible. As far as they're concerned, time is money.

A typical Virgo prefers to take a back seat rather than be in the front line. They feel uncomfortable if they have to spend too long in the spotlight, but they thrive on being a valued member of a support team or advisory committee. In fact, any way in which they can be of service will show them at their best. They should give themselves a well-deserved pat on the back!

Among the professions that are right up a Virgo's street are being an agent, accountant, secretary, teacher, writer, critic, scientist, doctor or nurse. A Virgo has a very enquiring mind, so needs a job that stretches their brain and lets them make the most of their considerable intellect. They'll hate any job that bores or stultifies them, or which doesn't make the most of their tremendous potential.

Although some Virgos are self-employed, most of them prefer the structure of working in an environment with other people. They also like the security of knowing they'll receive regular payments and may prefer this to the erratic earnings that can come with self-employment.

Money

Emotions may make a Virgo feel uncomfortable but they certainly don't muck about when it comes to money. The combination of the Virgo's Earth element and their intelligent planetary ruler, Mercury, makes them a formidable number-cruncher. They like to keep track of where they stand financially, and even if that doesn't always happen in reality they'll keep promising themselves that they're going to pull their socks up any minute now.

It's not that Virgos are miserly; they just don't like wasting money. You certainly couldn't accuse them of being spendthrifts. They don't exactly make Scrooge look open-handed but they do need to know that every penny they spend has been accounted for. A typical Virgo has a good eye for a bargain and doesn't feel happy about splashing out on frivolous luxuries or little treats – they rarely believe that they deserve such fripperies. They also enjoy tracking down a bargain and being very careful shoppers. The people you see in supermarkets tapping numbers into their calculators in order to compare the value of similar items are probably Virgos! When they can be bothered, they'll also cut money-saving coupons out of magazines.

When a Virgo needs to spend money on anything important or expensive, they won't jump into it on a whim. Instead, they'll spend a lot of time weighing up the pros and cons beforehand. They will probably also do a lot of research to make sure they buy the right model and will question the salesperson at length – woe betide them if they don't have all the answers!

If a Virgo wants to invest some money, they'll be happiest if they can seek some sound financial advice first. They are reluctant to take any kind of risk, so will prefer to know that their capital is growing steadily rather than in volatile fits and starts.

Health

This is another area in which Virgos really come into their

own. Every sign has a favourite hobby, and health is a big preoccupation for many Virgos. At best, a Virgo is very interested in staying healthy and is always keen to ensure they're eating the best possible diet and are getting plenty of exercise. They treat their body like a sophisticated machine that needs a lot of care and maintenance. They're also fascinated by its workings. At worst, they're a bit of a hypochondriac whose favourite bedtime reading is a medical encyclopaedia – then they can lie awake all night worrying about all the ailments they obviously have, from acne to zits.

Stress and anxiety are definitely among the biggest health challenges for a Virgo. If the government handed out gold medals for worrying, their mantelpiece would be groaning under the weight of them all. Once a Virgo starts to fret, their sensitive digestive system (which is ruled by this sign) begins to get snarled up, leading to stomach upsets, constipation and irritable bowels. Stress can also play havoc with other areas of their health, so it's important for them to work it off with plenty of exercise and fresh air. And it's vitally important that a Virgo learns to relax! Meditation can be very good for them because it encourages them to observe themselves and sit still – many Virgos spend lots of time dashing hither and thither, with barely time to sit down for a meal.

It's essential for a Virgo to eat food that suits their metabolism, and very often they benefit from a wholefood, organic or vegetarian diet. Not only does this help their vulnerable digestion to work more efficiently, it also makes them feel much more energetic and less tired.

The World of Virgo

Cities	Bath, Boston, Paris, Jerusalem, Strasbourg
Countries	Brazil, Switzerland, Turkey, West Indies
Colours	Navy blue, green, dark brown
Number	Five
Day of the week	Wednesday
Gemstone	Aquamarine
Crystal	Obsidian
Animals	All domestic pets
Foods	Barley, oats, root vegetables, rye
Plants	Buttercup, forget-me-not, speedwell
Tarot card	The Hermit

Compatibility

Virgo with Aries

This is one of the most difficult pairings of all. They're so different and want such different things out of life! The painstaking Virgo despairs of the impulsive Arien, who often seems to leap from crisis to crisis with great enthusiasm. They also find their lusty and passionate Arien too hot to handle for long.

Virgo with Taurus

There's a strong rapport between these two. It may not be the sort of relationship that will set the world alight but they both enjoy the comfortable predictability of it. They both know where they stand, which is so important to them. Some of the sexual games suggested by the naughty Virgo will shock the rather staid Taurean but they'll play along!

Virgo with Gemini

This is a meeting of minds. In some respects they're very

different and in others they have a lot in common, which gives them plenty to talk about. They're more comfortable as friends or business partners than they are as lovers, because their contrasting emotional styles can lead to misunderstandings and pain.

Virgo with Cancer

There's a lot to be said for this combination, although it often works best as friends. The Virgo appreciates the caring qualities of their Cancerian but can sometimes feel as though they're losing their independence. They also struggle to meet the Cancerian's powerful emotional needs because they simply don't understand them.

Virgo with Leo

This is a difficult combination. The naturally modest Virgo is often baffled and even slightly shocked by the Leo's leanings towards conspicuous consumption and possibly even outright swank. They also find it hard to tolerate the way their Leo dramatizes situations. It's all too much for the practical and sensible Virgo to tolerate for long.

Virgo with Virgo

Although no one understands a Virgo like another Virgo, this can be a rather tepid combination. Ideally, one if not both of the Virgos needs to be much more emotional than usual to prevent the relationship becoming mired in reservations and modesty. They can talk all they want, but need to find an emotional meeting ground as well.

Virgo with Libra

These two are much happier as friends than lovers because this helps to prevent bad feelings and hurt. The ever practical Virgo can help the Libran to get their life together and will encourage them to reach decisions. Virgo enjoys the Libran's intellectual abilities but can become suspicious of their charm and diplomacy. Are they really that nice?, they wonder.

Virgo with Scorpio

There's an endless fascination between these two signs. They both enjoy analysing what makes other people tick and they have plenty of scope with each other's fascinating foibles. The trouble can start if they allow their relationship to become too analytical and they forget about expressing their feelings. Sexually, it's dynamite!

Virgo with Sagittarius

Here's a tricky one. They enjoy talking and admire one another's brainpower, but the Virgo will quickly become annoyed by the Sagittarian's apparent inability to stick to the facts. They'll correct their Sagittarian every time they start to exaggerate and it will soon drive a wedge between them. They're better friends than lovers.

Virgo with Capricorn

These people understand one another. They share the need for an ordered life that runs as smoothly as possible. So what if it's slightly boring – at least it feels safe. The Virgo heartily admires the Capricorn's respect for the power of money and they also approve of the Capricorn's ability to be a workhorse. In the bedroom, they're surprisingly hot stuff.

Virgo with Aquarius

Both these people have very strong opinions and they're eager to tell each other all about them. They fare much better as friends than as lovers, because then their long conversations won't get in the way of the action. If they are lovers, the Virgo will soon feel frustrated by the Aquarian's take-it-or-leave-it attitude to sex.

Virgo with Pisces

This is a difficult combination. The Virgo prides themselves on being pragmatic and sensible, so is driven to distraction by the Piscean's chaotic way of life. They also quickly lose patience if the Piscean apparently lurches from crisis to crisis. The Virgo's suggestions of ways to improve things are seen by the Piscean as criticism.

LIBRA

24 September – 22 October

The Libra Personality

When you meet a Libran for the first time, your overriding impression will be of someone who is charming, diplomatic and eager to put you at your ease. They'll work hard to create a harmonious atmosphere and do whatever they can to help you.

Harmony is very important for members of this sign. They can't bear it when tempers are frayed or the atmosphere is tense, and they won't relax until things are back on an even keel. This sign is symbolized by the scales, and all Librans strive to create balance in their lives. But this doesn't mean their scales are always level. Instead, they fluctuate wildly up and down, with the Libran desperately trying to control the situation. They like to find a happy medium and to strike the right note at difficult moments.

It's very calming and relaxing to be around a Libran, even if they're a knot of tension inside. Part of this is thanks to their ability to put other people first and themselves second, so you always feel special. You also feel that they truly appreciate your company – and how can you resist someone like that? They have the gift of making you feel you're the only person in the world all the while they're talking to you. However, you may be surprised to see them treating everyone else in the same way!

Librans can thank their planetary ruler, Venus, for their megadose of charm. Venus ensures they rarely put a foot wrong. It also ensures that they usually look good. Tradition says that Libra is one of the best-looking signs in the zodiac – an accolade shared with Taurus which is also ruled by Venus. Librans certainly like to look their best and can put a lot of effort into their appearance. They have instinctive good taste and as they get older they prefer classic clothes to the latest fashion.

Although Librans have a reputation for being charm on legs, there's quite a tough side to them. Some astrologers say that a Libran is really an Arien on their best behaviour, as you may discover when you do something that annoys them. They will find ways of letting you know that they aren't pleased, and these can be quite surprising. For instance, forget the idea that a Libran never loses their temper. It's healthy for them to let off steam and the eruption is usually far less tempestuous if they allow themselves frequent outbursts. They are also good at being grumpy, subtly implying that if only you had behaved differently they wouldn't have to be so annoyed with you.

Libra

Libra is one of the three Air signs, which means they are happiest operating on an intellectual level. The combination of peace-loving Venus, who makes them reluctant to hurt people, and their brainy element of Air, means they always see at least two sides to every story and would rather sit on the fence than make up their minds. Is it any wonder that they're known for their indecision?

Love

This is one area of life where Librans do really well. The sign of Libra rules partnerships of all kinds, from passionate to platonic, including open enmity. In fact, Librans have such a powerful need for other people that they can feel like a fish out of water if they have to spend too long on their own. Their ready charm ensures their popularity and they can be extremely affectionate, loving and romantic. People find it hard to resist them!

A Libran is much happier in a relationship than out of one, so it's very difficult for them to cope with the prospect of splitting up from a long-term partner. They will endure a lot of misery and heartache rather than make the final break and be left on their own. This means they prefer to stay in a dead-end relationship than risk being left on the shelf. Very often, it's a Libran's partner who instigates the break.

It's very easy for other people to hurt a Libran's feelings, although they'll do their best to put on a brave face. Romance is the Libran's Achilles heel and it can break a Libran's heart over and over again. Some Librans can fall in love with love, perhaps because they're so keen to find a soulmate. They are also very idealistic and prefer to see only the good in other people. They will turn a blind eye to their partner's faults. When they do find a special someone, they tend to put them on a pedestal, looking up to them and inevitably feeling crushed and disappointed when this person reveals that they're human after all. Sadly, there are times when someone hurts a Libran but they come straight back for more – it's as if they can't learn from the experience.

Career

A typical Libran enjoys the high life, which means they need plenty of money to be able to afford it. As a result, unless they're lucky enough to have been left a fortune or they've had a big win on the Lottery, they need a good job that brings in lots of cash and, preferably, a few perks such as an expense account (which they'll enjoy using) and an attractive car.

Pleasant surroundings are very important to a Libran, so ideally they should work in a comfortable and pleasing environment – anything too Spartan or tacky will turn them off fast. It's also important for them to feel happy with their colleagues, because they'll hate coming into work if there's a tense atmosphere or the threat of a row always hanging in the air. Librans can't bear workmates who are nit-pickers or troublemakers. Such people may even make a Libran feel ill.

Even so, don't make the mistake of thinking that a Libran is a pushover at work. They're not! They can be surprisingly tough when the stakes are high enough and can drive a hard deal, although they usually lack the killer instinct that would make them a formidable opponent.

In a perfect world, a Libran should be part of a team. Working on their own doesn't suit them, partly because they quickly feel lonely and partly because it can be difficult to motivate themselves sometimes. They would be the first to admit that they prefer drinking coffee and eating biscuits to doing an unpleasant task. They are also not very good at keeping track of systems and being organized, because they tend to postpone anything tedious or difficult for another day. And, of course, that day rarely arrives!

Any job that makes the most of a Libran's charm and intellect will bring out the best in them. Professions that are particularly good for Librans include diplomacy, fashion, beauty and music.

Money

This is a very important part of any Libran's life because they need lots and lots of money. After all, they've got to pay for all the luxuries that they love, so it's no surprise that money has a habit of slipping through their fingers. There are so many things to spend it on, and so many temptations, that their biggest worry is deciding what to buy first. The arrival of their second worry usually coincides with that of their credit card or bank statement (provided they can bring themselves to open the envelope in the first place), but that's another story and one that they're probably all too familiar with. (And it's not helped by their inbuilt reluctance to confront anything unpleasant or ugly, so they'll tell themselves that things are a lot better than they imagine.)

A Libran enjoys spending their money on items that will bring pleasure to them and their loved ones, especially if that means arranging a big treat for everyone. However, it's essential that the Libran avoids any tendency to lavish presents on people because they want to buy their affection, rather than because they want to make them happy.

Occasionally you will meet a Libran who uses a combination of charm and cash to get what they want, thinking that everyone else has their price. Not only does this cause resentment in the person who is being bought, the Libran is probably fooling themselves about their motives, telling themselves that they're being generous out of the goodness of their heart. When this is thrown back in their face, they'll be full of righteous indignation that does nothing to help the situation. It is far better for a Libran to be honest about what they want, and to trust that people will love them for themselves rather than their spending power.

Health

Librans are very healthy on the whole. However, their enjoyment of the good life makes it easy for them to put on weight. It's one of the disadvantages of being ruled by Venus – this planet bestows good looks, immense charm and a beautiful voice, but also makes its subjects prone to piling on the pounds. Mind you, the fact that most Librans have a sweet tooth and enjoy eating rich foods won't help much either. The best antidote to this is plenty of exercise but, unless the Libran is very unusual, the thought of this doesn't exactly make them want to put down that doughnut, leap off the sofa and put on their jogging kit. They need a little encouragement.

Everyone benefits from some form of exercise, so the Libran should try to find a sport or activity that truly appeals to them, especially if they can combine it with a social activity, otherwise they'll never stick with it. Another secret to success is to make sure they exercise regularly and steadily – it's no good following a long period of inactivity with a hectic few hours in the gym because it will only leave them temporarily crippled and reluctant to have another go.

The area of the body ruled by Libra is the kidneys, so Librans need to keep an eye on any irregularities that are indicated by inexplicable headaches or backache. If their social life involves drinking a lot of alcohol, they should try to combat its effects with plenty of water and fruit juices to give their kidneys a chance to flush out all those toxins.

The World of Libra

Cities	Copenhagen, Frankfurt, Leeds, Vienna
Countries	Argentina, Austria, China, Japan, Tibet
Colours	Pastel blues and pinks
Number	Six
Day of the week	Friday
Gemstone	Sapphire
Crystal	Jade
Animal	Rabbit
Foods	Asparagus, chocolate, grapes
Plants	Ash tree, hydrangea, violet
Tarot card	Justice

Compatibility

Libra with Aries

When this couple first get together, they're intrigued by one another. Later on, however, the Libran is shocked by the Arien's self-centred attitude and the hot-headed way they lose their temper. Sexually, it can all become a bit too much for the gentle Libran if the Arien has an insatiable libido. The Libran may end up feeling like a sex object.

Libra with Taurus

This couple believe in enjoying themselves so they'll push the boat out at every opportunity. Their shared love of beauty brings them together, but the Libran will find it hard to cope if the Taurean is possessive or wants a very restrictive relationship. They may also clash over their differing intellectual needs.

Libra with Gemini

Here are two people who can really have a lot of fun together. The Libran appreciates the Gemini's lively mind and quick wit, and is delighted to be with someone who shares their high level of brainpower. Given time, they can encourage the Gemini to be more emotional and demonstrative, and to feel less embarrassed about bringing out their softer side.

Libra with Cancer

Both these people want to be happy. However, they can have differing views on what this means, with the Libran wanting peace at all costs and the Cancerian valuing family life above all else. The Libran might enjoy being with the Cancerian's family but will soon decide they can have too much of a good thing.

Libra with Leo

This is a show-stopping relationship. It can also have a pretty dramatic effect on the couple's finances, because neither sign likes to stint themselves. They'll egg each other on to enjoy the best that money can buy. Emotionally, they bring out the best in each other, although the Libran may find the Leo over-dramatic at times.

Libra with Virgo

Friendship is a much better bet than love for this couple. The Libran enjoys having the Virgo as a friend, and will benefit from their no-nonsense attitude. However, as a lover the Libran will feel perplexed and rather hurt by the

Virgo's slightly remote attitude. They have such different approaches to life that it's difficult to find any middle ground.

Libra with Libra

At last the Libran has found someone who truly appreciates them! They enjoy taking care of one another and will spend many happy hours shopping, eating and generally having as good a time as possible. It won't take much for them to live beyond their means but they won't really care because it's all so much fun.

Libra with Scorpio

This is a difficult pairing because they simply don't understand one another. Although the Libran could learn a lot from the Scorpio's ability to immerse themselves in their emotions, they can't bear the thought of losing control like that. The Scorpio's passionate approach to sex can also be too strong for the Libran to tolerate.

Libra with Sagittarius

Expect plenty of laughs when these two get together. The Libran enjoys the Sagittarian's natural optimism, enthusiasm and good humour, and also likes being with someone who's a match for them intellectually. They'll spend many happy hours talking about all sorts of subjects. Emotionally, they have a good rapport.

Libra with Capricorn

This is a good business partnership, provided the Libran is prepared to match the Capricorn's round-the-clock working pattern. However, it can be an uneasy emotional relationship because the Libran is often disconcerted by the Capricorn's rather distant and reserved attitude. They can misconstrue this as lack of interest.

Libra with Aquarius

What a great combination! This couple enjoy each other's company and really benefit from being together. The Libran may even learn to be more decisive, thanks to the Aquarian's cut-and-dried opinions. Intellectually, this is a marvellous match. Emotionally, it's got a lot going for it, provided the Aquarian is happy to show their feelings.

Libra with Pisces

These are the two great romantics of the zodiac, so you can expect plenty of hearts and flowers. They have a lot in common, both preferring to ignore anything nasty in life. However, this can cause problems if it means they both turn a blind eye to the difficulties in their relationship. They should encourage each other to be more realistic.

SCORPIO

23 October – 22 November

Scorpio

The Scorpio Personality

As far as some people are concerned, being a Scorpio is only one step removed from being a social outcast and someone to be avoided at all costs. Scorpios often wince when they reveal their sign, expecting the other person to back away, make their excuses and leave. Too often they're reminded that Scorpios are supposed to be everyone else's worst nightmare.

Do Scorpios really deserve their reputation for being emotional volcanoes, back-stabbers and walking sex bombs? (And that's when they're on their best behaviour!) No, of course they don't! Yes, you will sometimes encounter a Scorpio who has lost their way and is living out all the worst traits of this sign, but the vast majority of Scorpios are much more restrained and balanced. They are also terrific company and have a fantastic sense of humour!

Scorpios certainly view life in a very emotional and intense way, thanks to their Water element. However, because they're ruled by the planet Pluto, which is named after the god of the underworld and hidden riches, they find it very difficult to express these profound feelings. They are there all right but they're buried under the surface, and a Scorpio's innate need for privacy and secrecy makes them reluctant to let people know how they feel. Perhaps that's one of the reasons so many bad characteristics are projected on to Scorpios – people always tend to exaggerate what they're frightened or unsure of.

This sign is often accused of being obsessive – it's true that a Scorpio takes things very seriously, but only when their powerful energies have become so blocked that they develop a one-track mind. However, when that happens they can be quite obsessive about things. They're happiest when they're able to concentrate their energies in particular directions, because they need to feel emotionally involved in everything they do. Otherwise, life loses its meaning and purpose.

Once a Scorpio has made up their mind about something it is very hard to persuade them to change it. They often have fixed ideas about all sorts of things and can take a very hard line over such topics as capital punishment and imprisonment. It must be said that despite a Scorpio's natural loyalty, if you push them too far or double-cross them in some way, they will never forget it and they will never forgive you. This will be made more than apparent because they will probably give you the cold shoulder or find other ways to exact their revenge. It's wise not to get on the wrong side of a Scorpio!

A Scorpio's magnetic charm and powerful personality attract many fans. People love the idea that still waters run deep, and while a Scorpio maintains their inscrutable silence everyone else will be wondering what they're really thinking, and will go to great lengths to find out. They know there's a lot more going on under the surface than the Scorpio will ever reveal.

Love

This is an area of life that can cause problems for a Scorpio because they take it so seriously. There's nothing superficial about members of this sign, and as a result they need relationships that are deep and satisfying. A Scorpio has to be truly involved in their partnerships otherwise they simply don't work. One-night stands and brief flirtations quickly lose their charm – they're looking for something more significant than that, and when they find it they'll channel all their energies into it. They demand a great deal from their partner, with love and loyalty at the top of the list. After all, these are qualities that the Scorpio is prepared to bring to the relationship themselves, so they expect the same in return.

One big Scorpio problem is jealousy, and another is possessiveness. It can be very difficult for a Scorpio to resolve these issues, especially if they've been hurt in the past and now feel reluctant to trust people. Whenever they feel vulnerable they will want their partner to account for their every action and to reassure the Scorpio that they aren't about to go off with someone else. Although we all feel insecure and need reassurance at times, too much of this will soon backfire on the Scorpio and they may even find that they bring about the very situation they've been fearing. Their partner may get so fed up that they deliberately give the Scorpio something to feel jealous about.

Sex and Scorpio go together like bread and butter. Most Scorpios place a great importance on sex because it's such a good way for them to express their feelings. It also helps them to release a lot of pent-up nervous tension. However, since Scorpios have an all-or-nothing approach to life, sometimes you'll meet a Scorpio who completely avoids sex, probably because they've had some nasty experiences and aren't keen on repeating them. But this is the exception that proves the rule!

Career

Whatever a Scorpio does for a living, it must have meaning and purpose for them. As with every other area of their life, they need to feel emotionally involved in their career. If they don't, they'll feel unhappy, dissatisfied and as though an important element is missing from their life. They must also believe that their work is worthy of their time and effort. They will feel wretched if what they do for a living is demeaning or boring. If they are a typical Scorpio they'll pour all their energies into their work, so they want something that provides endless interest and stimulation and which also gives them a sense of purpose.

Scorpios always like to know what's going on so they are the eyes and ears of most offices and factories. They love intrigue and enjoy knowing the latest gossip.

Scorpios are far more sensitive than they let on, so it's important that they get on well with their colleagues and work in a comfortable atmosphere. Scorpios also need to be given a position of power, even if this is quite minor. They will be very unhappy if they think everyone else is wielding control but they are powerless.

A Scorpio is unlikely to be attracted to jobs that are

frivolous, superficial or tedious – they'll quickly become bored and, if there's no other option on the horizon, resentful of what Fate has dumped in their lap. Any career that enables them to examine situations in depth – something that Scorpios are particularly good at – is ideal for them, so they could be attracted to detective work, the law, science (peering down a microscope will enthral them), medicine, research or mining. They'll also get great satisfaction from working in the wine trade – especially if they can attend lots of wine-tastings.

Money

Everyone needs money in order to survive, but Scorpios need it more than most. Financial security is very important to them – they need to know that a steady flow of money is coming into their bank account, so any interruptions to it will make them feel nervous and worried. It has to be said that they also like to have money because of the power it gives them – and power is very important to Scorpios. Of course, this power can come in many forms. They may enjoy knowing that they've got more money than their friends, or they may get great satisfaction from knowing that money enables them to live comfortably and enjoy themselves. If they have enough money, they try to give some of it to a good cause.

Sometimes, a Scorpio will try to use money to buy power and control over other people. They will probably do this in a very subtle way and may not even be conscious of what they're doing. But they will place a lot of importance on status symbols, priding themselves on owning the biggest and most expensive car in the street. They may also mortgage themselves up to the hilt in order to live in the sort of house that their family and friends can only dream of.

If they have any cash to spare, a Scorpio likes the thought of investing it in stocks and shares – they enjoy knowing that those carefully-placed investments are slowly accumulating behind the scenes and they also like being linked with some of the world's biggest companies. They are canny investors and will enjoy playing the stock market. However, if they want to sleep soundly at night they should try not to put all their eggs in one basket or invest more money than they can afford to lose.

Health

The way we release our energies is important for all the signs, but especially so for a Scorpio. Because they tend to concentrate their energies and channel them in particular directions to the exclusion of all else, a Scorpio must make sure they don't become blocked or frustrated in any way. If they do, they could feel the effects physically, through strange illnesses or a deep sense of frustration. They may also suffer from problems with their genitals, which are ruled by Scorpio.

'Moderation in all things' is a good Scorpio motto, but whether members of this sign follow it is quite another matter. For a start, when they become involved in something they put their heart and soul into it, whether it's a love affair or their new passion for cricket. It's all or nothing for Scorpios. As a result, they mustn't overdo it when they take exercise – it'll be tempting for them to throw themselves into the activities to such an extent that they strain themselves and end up in a worse state than when they started. They should try to release their energies smoothly and steadily, and not alternate long periods of inactivity with protracted bouts of exercise.

This tendency to go overboard also extends to food and drink, and sometimes a Scorpio doesn't know when to stop. This means they can sometimes feel wretched due to a crushing hangover or after eating too much rich food. Their sensitive digestive system is usually affected, causing constipation or an upset stomach.

If a Scorpio does decide to take some more exercise, they could try something that allows them to move in a controlled yet powerful way, such as t'ai chi, yoga or one of the martial arts. It's easy for a Scorpio to bottle up problems, so if they choose an activity that also helps them to relax, so much the better.

The World of Scorpio

Cities	Baltimore, Cincinnati, Dover, Liverpool
Countries	Algeria, Egypt, Morocco, Syria
Colour	Dark red
Number	Eight
Day of the week	Tuesday
Gemstone	Opal
Crystal	Jasper
Animals	Eagle, phoenix, scorpion
Foods	Blackberry, garlic, onion
Plants	Hawthorn, heather, rhododendron
Tarot card	Death

Compatibility

Scorpio with Aries

There's plenty of heat and passion here. But the Scorpio likes to play their cards close to their chest and may find the Arien rather too direct and forthright for their taste. Sexually, lots of sparks will fly – and not only emotionally.

The Scorpio likes to be seduced but the Arien sometimes doesn't have time for such niceties.

Scorpio with Taurus

This is a happy couple! They have plenty in common but enough differences to keep life interesting. The Scorpio is always relieved when they know where they stand and this is more than likely with a straightforward, loyal Taurean. They both enjoy their home comforts and will happily create a cosy nest they can retreat to.

Scorpio with Gemini

This can be a mismatch. They have such contrasting ways of looking at life that they'll have to work hard to make their relationship a success. The Scorpio may be frustrated by the Gemini's apparently superficial attitude and may also suspect them of being flighty and flirty.

Scorpio with Cancer

This relationship has a lot of sticking power. Neither of these people is interested in short-term partnerships so they'll invest a lot of effort into staying together. The Scorpio will appreciate being looked after so well by their Cancerian. The only problem that may arise is if the Scorpio is very secretive and it makes the Cancerian feel threatened.

Scorpio with Leo

It's a dramatic performance when these two get together. They both believe in living life to the full and their relationship won't be without its tempestuous moments. For a start, both of them always believe they're right! But at least their relationship is full of passion – something that they both need if they're to feel completely fulfilled.

Scorpio with Virgo

This couple get on well together and they admire each other's no-nonsense qualities. They're instinctive friends but there are enough differences between them to ensure there's always something to talk about. The Scorpio is intrigued by the contrast between the Virgo's modest public image and what happens behind the bedroom door.

Scorpio with Libra

As friends, this unlikely couple will manage to see the best in each other. But it's a different story when they're lovers because they're chalk and cheese. The Scorpio is soon irritated by the peace-loving Libran. Why can't they lose their temper once in a while? The Scorpio will also be annoyed by the Libran's insistence on fair play. It spoils the fun!

Scorpio with Scorpio

Too much of a good thing? It might be when two Scorpios get together. They understand one another only too well, which of course has many benefits. Emotionally, they're on cloud nine. However, it's horribly easy for them to absorb each other's bad moods, so the atmosphere can swiftly turn from sunshine to storms.

Scorpio with Sagittarius

What's going with these two? Probably a lot of misunderstandings! This couple are better as friends or business partners than as lovers because their emotional needs are so different. The Scorpio will be instantly suspicious if the Sagittarian wants an independent social life. Also, their intense passion will overwhelm the Sagittarian.

Scorpio with Capricorn

It's a strange pairing but it can work! This couple share a need to be seen to do well, so the Scorpio will understand the Capricorn's workaholic tendencies and enjoy the material results. Sexually, it's a pretty earthy combination. The only problem comes if the Scorpio can't encourage the Capricorn to open up emotionally.

Scorpio with Aquarius

This is a tricky one! Although they respect one another's intellects, this couple will struggle to stay together. The Scorpio is resentful and suspicious of the Aquarian's streak of independence because they can't understand or control it. They will also fall out because they're both opinionated and convinced that they're in the right!

Scorpio with Pisces

Provided that the Scorpio is ready to show their softer side and the Piscean is keen to develop their tougher side, this couple will be happy together. Problems come if the Piscean is weak-willed and allows the Scorpio to bully them. Nevertheless, they'll both enjoy the intense emotional relationship that develops between them.

SAGITTARIUS

23 November – 21 December

Sagittarius

The Sagittarius Personality

One of the greatest things about a Sagittarian is their irrepressible optimism. They are blessed with the complete conviction that everything will work out for the best. Even when things become dicey and they start to worry, it won't be long before the Sagittarian begins to feel positive again. This is one of their greatest strengths and it has helped them to weather many storms. No matter how tough things are, a typical Sagittarian retains a positive attitude, their sense of humour and a strong belief that everything will be OK in the end. Of course, they have their bad days like everyone else, but eventually they will always find the silver lining in the cloud. Perhaps this resilient attitude to trouble is the reason that Sagittarius is said to be the luckiest sign in the zodiac!

It's Jupiter, the planetary ruler of Sagittarius, that gives members of this sign such a life-enhancing attitude. Jupiter is the planet of good fortune and challenges. Sagittarius is the third of the Fire signs, which makes its subjects expansive, enthusiastic and always keen to take the initiative and make things happen. And they certainly do that! It's a rare Sagittarian who likes to sit around for long, watching the grass grow. Although even these balls of fire need to rest every now and then, they aren't happy unless they've got an exciting new project on the go. If they haven't, they will soon start to feel fed up and possibly even depressed, because they don't have anything to aim for.

Goals are very important for Sagittarians. The sign is symbolized by the Archer shooting his arrows into the air. In the same way, a typical Sagittarian has always got their eye on a target – usually slightly out of their reach, because where's the fun in achieving something simple? A Sagittarian always prefers a challenge to a walkover! Once they've achieved their goal, they'll have their eye on the next target.

Life is always lively when a Sagittarian is around. They enjoy discussing ideas with friends and loved ones, especially if the conversations involve a favourite topic or have philosophical, spiritual or political overtones. A Sagittarian is very intellectual and enjoys stretching their mind, so they probably have a home full of books and an extremely broad range of knowledge. They have a tremendous respect for knowledge and they spend their lives learning more about people and the world around them.

Sagittarians always pride themselves on their honesty. They hate hypocrites and despise yes-men, so you can usually expect to hear the truth from them. However, this may not always be a comfortable experience! It doesn't help that a little exaggeration often sneaks into a Sagittarian's conversation. Somehow, the Sagittarian version of the truth often turns out to be blunter and more direct than you were expecting. It may also involve the Sagittarian dropping a clanger at the same time. Of all the members of the zodiac, Sagittarians are the ones most likely to suffer from foot in mouth disease.

Love

This is one of the most popular signs of the zodiac. People can't help flocking around Sagittarians – they appear to radiate a friendly, easygoing force-field. In addition to that, Sagittarians are terrific company and laughter never seems to be far away. No wonder they have a lot of friends.

People appreciate the open and straightforward manner of the Sagittarian because it means they know where they stand. After all, this is not exactly the most tactful sign in the zodiac so it's awkward for a Sagittarian to be anything other than honest – they're usually found out if they tell lies because they let the cat out of the bag sooner or later.

The one thing a Sagittarian can't abide is feeling tied down or hemmed in by a partner. They need to be able to lead their own life and not feel that someone is peering over their shoulder the whole time or trying to curb their freedom. If their partner is guilty of any of these transgressions, the Sagittarian won't tolerate it for long and will soon voice their objections. They may even end the relationship if that's the only way to maintain a sense of independence. If there are reasons why they can't leave their partner, they will start to distance themselves from them in an attempt to have a life of their own.

Although sex means a lot to a Sagittarian, because it allows them a lot of self-expression, the most important requirement when looking for a partner is someone who will be a friend as well as a lover. A Sagittarian needs a partner who'll still be their best friend long after the passion between them has simmered down, and whose intellect matches their own. Anything less simply isn't good enough.

Career

This is one of the most intellectual signs in the zodiac, so ideally a Sagittarian should choose a career that gives their brain plenty of scope and, preferably, presents a challenge. They hate the thought of a job that's dreary, monotonous or so mindless that they just switch off while they're doing it. Anything that smacks of routine will soon make them feel fed up. Instead, they need an occupation that allows them continually to learn more about the world and to add to their store of knowledge. Preferably, it should also involve plenty of changes of scene to stop them getting bored.

A Sagittarian is a very sociable creature so ideally they need to be surrounded by lively colleagues. They aren't very keen on working alone for long stretches at a time – they will soon find ways to distract themselves, such as phoning a friend or doing research on the Internet (which really means surfing all their favourite websites). They are usually popular among their workmates because of their knack of livening up the atmosphere and making people laugh.

A Sagittarian is a born teacher, so if they can impart some of their experience to other people – even in very informal ways – they'll feel satisfied and content. They also need a job that keeps them on the move: being stuck behind a desk or permanently at a shop counter will soon start to frustrate them. If they can also meet plenty of interesting people in the course of their work, they'll be really happy.

Ideal Sagittarian professions include education, publishing, writing, broadcasting, religion, philosophy and travel. Although Sagittarians are not particularly ambitious, they do like to feel a sense of achievement and to know that they're getting a lot out of their work – and also that they're putting a lot into it.

Money

Sagittarians need plenty of this! They love spending money, so they need to earn it. Unfortunately, they're not very good at taking care of their cash so they may have a rather slapdash approach to finance. Tedious details such as the state of their bank balance or the ebb and flow of direct debits through their account are about as exciting as last week's news. The Sagittarian will tell themselves that they've got more important things to think about, although they sometimes face a monetary crisis and are forced to take action because something has gone skew-whiff.

As far as most Sagittarians are concerned, the most exciting thing about money is what it can buy. Books, for a start, since virtually every Sagittarian has a well-stocked library at home that they're always adding to. Another important Sagittarian hobby is travel, and many members of this sign enjoy globe-trotting. They love the thought of adventurous holidays to far-flung corners of the world, and will happily work hard in order to afford them.

Expensive possessions that act as status symbols don't usually appeal to Sagittarians – they can't be bothered with such things. They'll probably break or ruin them within a week, anyway! Most Sagittarians prefer wearing casual clothes to anything formal so aren't particularly impressed by designer labels. Even so, they may be prepared to spend a fortune on beautiful clothes made from leather and suede (although the inevitable and frequent dry cleaning bills will be high). They also enjoy buying accessories such as gloves, belts and hats, and the cost of all these can really mount up.

Sagittarians often have a weak spot when it comes to cars. Many Sagittarians would love to own a fast car that's sleek and very distinctive. It probably costs a fortune, too! A Sagittarian's ideal is to have enough money to be free to do whatever they want with their life.

Health

It doesn't take long before a Sagittarian starts to feel restless and edgy, especially if they have to spend hours in one place. This is one of the most active signs of all, so a typical Sagittarian enjoys being on the move. Even on days when they don't leave the house or office, they may get plenty of exercise simply because they find it hard to sit still and are always dashing from one room to another.

The more sedentary a Sagittarian's life, the more jittery they feel, although they're not always keen on taking exercise just for the sake of it. They need activities that engage their brain as well as their body. They enjoy walking, although their busy schedule may mean they spend more time in the car or behind a desk than pounding the pavements. It's important for a Sagittarian to reverse this trend whenever possible – they really benefit from being in wide open spaces and breathing plenty of fresh air. Among the activities that could appeal are horse-riding (this sign is noted for its love of horses), squash, motor-racing and any other sport that requires nerves of steel and a daredevil attitude. As a result, a Sagittarian can often strain muscles, especially if the pursuits they choose are dangerous or strenuous.

For a Sagittarian, the vulnerable areas of the body are the hips and liver. When they put on weight, it's most likely to centre around their hips and can be increasingly hard to shift as the years pass. They thoroughly enjoy eating and drinking, which means their liver can suffer, especially if they eat a lot of rich food. They need to combine all those gastronomic binges with a more restrained diet.

The World of Sagittarius

Cities	Budapest, Cologne, Nottingham, York
Countries	Arabia, Australia, Hungary, Spain
Colour	Purple
Number	Three
Day of the week	Thursday
Gemstone	Amber
Crystal	Turquoise
Animal	Horse
Foods	Celeriac, leek, onion,
Plants	Borage, carnation, dandelion, sage
Tarot card	Temperance

Compatibility

Sagittarius with Aries

This couple can look forward to lots of fun and games. They have a similar outlook on life, both wanting to enjoy it as much as possible. They also have plenty of interests in common. There's always a good-humoured sense of competitiveness to their relationship and they'll love spurring each other on to tackle fresh challenges.

Sagittarius with Taurus

It's hard to know what this couple see in each other. The freedom-loving Sagittarian will soon feel stifled by the security-loving Taurean. Any sexual or emotional relationship could soon founder. Even as friends, they will struggle to understand one another. The Sagittarian likes to live for today; the Taurean wants to save for tomorrow.

Sagittarius with Gemini

These people are soulmates! They can expect to have tremendous fun together, talking about everything under the sun. The Sagittarian will encourage the Gemini to concentrate on things in more depth than they're used to, and their warm affections will help the Gemini to relax and be more demonstrative than usual.

Sagittarius with Cancer

There are so many differences between these two that they'll battle to find any common ground. The Sagittarian needs to pull their punches when delivering home truths to the Cancerian, otherwise they'll have to endure a lot of hurt silences. The Sagittarian's need for room to breathe emotionally will confuse and upset the Cancerian.

Sagittarius with Leo

This is a terrific combination because these two have a lot in common. They're both very affectionate and demonstrative. They're also very keen to get as much out of life as possible, and will talk each other into all sorts of escapades. The Sagittarian will gently take the mickey out of the Leo whenever they get too big for their boots.

Sagittarius with Virgo

The major selling point for this partnership is fascination. Both people are intrigued by each other and there's always plenty to talk about. The only hitch will come if they're so busy talking that they rarely get around to the more intimate aspects of their relationship. However, as friends they really enjoy one another's company.

Sagittarius with Libra

Here's a couple that like to enjoy themselves. When they get together it's a licence to spend money because neither of them needs any encouragement to be extravagant. They'll have endless discussions in which they put the world to rights since they both have very strong opinions about morality and fair play.

Sagittarius with Scorpio

This is a strange relationship. The Sagittarian will at first be intrigued by the Scorpio's intensity and power, but the novelty value will soon start to pall. They stand a much better chance as friends than as lovers, because they have a lot to learn from each other about when to take things seriously and when to laugh things off.

Sagittarius with Sagittarius

This can be a noisy combination because Sagittarians enjoy talking and they also enjoy laughter. They are probably better friends than live-in lovers, simply because they're likely to see more of each other that way. They may both be so independent, with such busy social lives, that they're rarely at home at the same time.

Sagittarius with Capricorn

Opposites attract when this couple get together. The big question is whether they can surmount their massive differences and find some common ground. This can be hard work, especially if the Sagittarian is very optimistic and the Capricorn has a tendency to be pessimistic. They can help each other a lot, but are they willing to make the effort?

Sagittarius

Sagittarius with Aquarius

A relationship between these two is plenty of fun. They both pride themselves on being independent-minded, so there will be lots of heated discussions on a whole variety of topics. To onlookers, it may seem that their relationship is emotionally lightweight, but a solid core of love and affection binds them together.

Sagittarius with Pisces

This is a strange relationship. Things will go well if the Piscean is upbeat and positive but the Sagittarian will soon lose their patience if the Piscean is very moody and struggles to deal with the vagaries of life. The Sagittarian must curb their tendency to speak first and think later, otherwise they'll badly hurt the Piscean.

CAPRICORN

22 December – 20 January

The Capricorn Personality

It isn't always a lot of fun being a Capricorn; not because they aren't fun people (Capricorns are noted for their sense of humour), but because other people don't think much of this sign. They dismiss it as boring, dull or too dutiful for words.

Well, it's about time all that ended! We have all met Capricorns who are full of depressingly bleak pronouncements, such as that the light at the end of the tunnel is an oncoming train. But usually a Capricorn is terrific company and the perfect person to turn to in a crisis. In fact, their wonderful sense of humour is frequently their saving grace. Not only does it help them to put problems in perspective, but anyone who's enjoyed a good laugh with a Capricorn will always want to come back for more. Who wouldn't?

Another of Capricorn's greatest strengths is the ability to learn from experience. Some signs make the same errors over and over again but it's an unusual Capricorn who can't turn a bad mistake into a valuable lesson sooner or later. This is important, because it's rare to find a Capricorn who goes through life unscathed. Most of them have their crosses to bear but they usually grit their teeth and get on with it. This endurance and sticking power stays with them through life.

They have Saturn, their planetary ruler, to thank for this. Saturn is the planet of hard knocks and tough experiences, so is a tough taskmaster. Saturn rules limitations, and sometimes a Capricorn will seem hidebound and hemmed in by their own lack of confidence. Certainly, some Capricorns are very shy, but as they grow up they usually learn to live with their natural reserve.

Saturn also gives the typical Capricorn a rather pessimistic view of life. Their glass is always half-empty, never half-full. Sometimes they feel that something awful is waiting to happen. If their gloomy premonitions are proved correct, the Capricorn can become quite depressed. They may also be quite fearful about the future and need to find a sympathetic listener so they can unburden themselves. That is, provided they are willing to show themselves in a vulnerable light.

You see, reputation is very important to Capricorns. They want to be seen in a good light at all times by everyone, from the next-door neighbour to their boss. Perhaps this is why they often dress quite formally, as though they'll let themselves down if they wear anything very casual. They like to wear blacks and greys so they can blend into the background whenever they want some protective colouring.

Capricorns were born with another wonderful bonus that the rest of the Sun signs don't have. All the other signs age as they get older, but the reverse happens for Capricorns. Very often a typical Capricorn starts out with an old head on young shoulders, making them look and act much older than they really are. Yet, as they grow older, the normal ageing process goes into reverse and they somehow become younger. They mellow, learn to relax and can be quite skittish by middle age. By the time old age comes along, they can make teenagers look positively boring!

Love

The most important thing to remember is that a Capricorn always wants to give a good impression and look as though they are in control. They may seem calm and collected on the surface but they're not nearly as emotionally unruffled as they appear. Deep down, they're extremely shy and vulnerable.

A Capricorn's feelings are easily hurt, even if they don't let on, and over the years they may learn to distance themselves emotionally from people as a form of protection. Yet that doesn't stop them feeling things deeply, even if they can't bring themselves to show it. In fact, Capricorns aren't noted for their demonstrative affections and they can feel quite shy about letting people know how they feel. What happens if they're rebuffed or rejected? they wonder. How will they cope? So they try to avoid emotional scenes and may even shy away from close relationships altogether, so they don't run the risk of being hurt. Unfortunately, this attitude can cause difficulties with loved ones, who mistake the Capricorn's reserve for indifference. The Capricorn should make sure their loved ones know that they are cared for, even if the Capricorn can't always show it.

Although Capricorns can be quite solitary creatures, they benefit tremendously from being in a loving relationship. Their partner can help them to unwind at the end of a long day and may also encourage them to be more demonstrative and openly affectionate. Most Capricorns have a rather traditional view of long-term relationships, even when they're young. The men may believe they should be the breadwinners, and the women may want to stay at home and look after the family.

Capricorn

Despite a Capricorn's reserved image, they can be hot stuff in the bedroom – an earth sign that can be very earthy indeed in the right circumstances!

Career

This is where Capricorns really come into their own. They need to be taken seriously by the world and they have a strong sense of their direction in life. They consider their career to be a way of proving themselves and they devote a lot of time to it. Yet they may have several false starts or feel that they aren't getting very far at first. That's because life is often a struggle for Capricorns until they reach their thirtieth birthdays, after which things become much easier and their careers begin to take off.

Whatever a Capricorn's age, their job is very important to them because they need to prove that they're a success and can make their own way through life. They're extremely ambitious and may have secret plans about heading straight for the top of their particular tree. What's more, they stand an excellent chance of succeeding, no matter how long it takes.

At work, a Capricorn is an invaluable member of a team, thanks to their diligence, pragmatism and patience.

Bosses and colleagues know they can rely on the Capricorn to get things done – they won't let the side down. This strong sense of duty can keep a Capricorn chained to their desk long after everyone else has gone home, and can quickly turn them into a workaholic. Their family life may suffer, but the Capricorn still can't imagine behaving in any other way.

This means that a Capricorn without a goal in life is a very sorry sight. If they are out of work for long they will soon become depressed and lacking in self-confidence. They will also feel it's all their fault.

Among the professions that are ideally suited to a Capricorn are big business, dentistry, osteopathy, the civil service and government work. They cope well with responsible jobs, and even if it is lonely at the top they'll be able to manage beautifully.

Money

Capricorns have a healthy respect for money and what it can buy. It's no coincidence that there are many jokes about the Capricorn streak of meanness. Members of this sign like to make sure that every penny is accounted for. They certainly don't like to fritter money away, although once they're well-heeled they can be surprisingly open-handed when making major purchases. Mind you, the Capricorn will still be reluctant to part with small amounts of cash – the person who drives from one supermarket to the next in the quest for the cheapest prices is usually a Capricorn.

Money also means a lot to a Capricorn because it offers them material and emotional security and, therefore, the respect of others. These are the essential ingredients of a Capricorn's happiness and they will feel something is missing if they don't have all three. The Capricorn will be reluctant to get married or start a family until they know they can afford to do so – they hate the thought of a hand-to-mouth existence and will work round the clock to ensure they earn enough money to live comfortably.

When investing that hard-earned cash, a Capricorn likes to buy things that will last a long time. Generally speaking, fads and fashions pass them by because the Capricorn knows these won't last so there is no point in wasting precious money on them. What the Capricorn is looking for are durability and quality. They have a natural affinity with big business so may become interested in dabbling in the stock market, but only if they're certain there's little risk of losing their shirt.

Health

One of the biggest bugbears for a Capricorn is their ability to worry. They'll worry about anything given half the chance. And if they don't have anything to worry about, they'll worry that they've forgotten something important! Either way it can lead to sleepless nights, poor digestion and a persistent sense of impending doom.

This is partly because Capricorns have such a strong sense of responsibility, thanks to their strict ruler, Saturn. For instance, it is hard for them to flop on the sofa if a pile of washing-up is waiting for them in the sink. Learning to relax properly has a dramatic impact on their energy levels and will also improve their sleeping patterns. If a Capricorn finds it hard to unwind, they should get involved in a hobby that will allow them to keep active while engaging their mind – gardening suits them well, because contact with the ground complements their Earth element and they also benefit from being in the fresh air. However, yet again, they need to combat the nagging feeling that they can't knock off for the day until they've eradicated every weed from the garden.

The body's skeletal structure is ruled by Capricorn, so members of this sign need to take care of their bones in general and their knees in particular. Ideally, they should live in a warm, dry climate because they're very vulnerable to the cold and damp. Unfortunately, Capricorns can be susceptible to arthritis, so they should take plenty of gentle exercise to prevent becoming stiff and seizing up. They can also have problems with their teeth, so need to find a sympathetic dentist.

The World of Capricorn

Cities	Brussels, Delhi, Frankfurt am Main, Oxford
Countries	Albania, Bulgaria, India, Mexico
Colour	Grey, Black
Number	Four
Day of the week	Saturday
Gemstone	Topaz
Crystal	Lapis lazuli
Animal	Goat
Foods	Barley, meat, spinach
Plants	Ivy, pansy, yew tree
Tarot card	The Devil

Compatibility

Capricorn with Aries

These people are very good for each other! The Arien teaches the Capricorn not to take life so seriously and to relax more. Even so, there is an element of friendly competition, especially in their careers, that can lead to success for both of them and a very comfortable standard of living.

Capricorn with Taurus

This partnership places a big emphasis on security. Both signs like to feel safe in a relationship and to know that their hearts won't be broken. If anything, this couple can appear to be rather conservative and staid, possibly with the relationship seeming old-fashioned. But it's probably pretty spicy when they're in private!

Capricorn with Gemini

This is often a short-lived relationship because these people have little in common. The Capricorn will enjoy being around the lively Gemini but their heavy workload may eventually spoil things between them. They're good friends because they're able to enjoy their profound differences rather than struggle to surmount them.

Capricorn with Cancer

Here's a relationship that can happily stand the test of time and will become even more satisfying as the years roll by. Both people need emotional security and they'll work hard to make one another feel safe. The Capricorn may even be encouraged to be less reserved and more openly demonstrative. They can let their guard down with a Cancerian.

Capricorn with Leo

Both signs place a lot of importance on outward appearances, so occasionally this partnership may be all style and little substance. They are often happier as business partners than as lovers, because they both have a healthy respect for money. The Capricorn can work behind the scenes while the Leo fronts the operation.

Capricorn with Virgo

This is a relationship where both partners know where they stand. And that's exactly how they like it because neither of them wants to waste their time or be left guessing. Their partnership may seem to be lacking in open affection and, as time goes on, it can become more like a business relationship than an emotional one.

Capricorn with Libra

Although these two have enough in common to bring them together, it may not be enough to keep them together for long. The Capricorn may find that the Libran isn't assertive enough and will soon be irritated by their desire to find the happy medium whenever possible. They'll do better as friends or colleagues.

Capricorn with Scorpio

Everything goes on underneath the surface with this couple. They will give the impression of being rather detached and distant but there will be some hot and heavy scenes in private. They both enjoy a high standard of living and will work hard to achieve it. This may mean that their relationship places a lot of emphasis on money and what it can buy.

Capricorn with Sagittarius

It isn't exactly plain sailing when these two pair up. They may well hit squalls if the Capricorn disapproves of the Sagittarian's lifestyle or wants them to spend more time at home. On the plus side, however, there will be plenty of laughter and the Capricorn may learn to be more relaxed and less uptight. Even so, the relationship requires lots of hard slog.

Capricorn with Capricorn

At last a Capricorn has found someone who understands them! The question is whether they're too similar. Ideally, they should both appreciate their home comforts, otherwise they'll spend all their spare time working and will never see one another. As business partners, they make a formidable team. Watch out, world!

Capricorn with Aquarius

This is a strange combination because they're so different. The Capricorn has a sentimental attachment to tradition while the Aquarius wants to sweep it away and deal with the facts. So will this relationship work? They need to find some common ground otherwise they'll wind each other up and become infuriated with one another.

Capricorn with Pisces

This can work, provided the Capricorn brings out their innate kindness and the Piscean displays their common sense. They have a lot to teach each other. The Capricorn sees that it's acceptable to be emotional and the Piscean learns to be more self-reliant. Even so, they will have to work hard to make allowances for one another.

AQUARIUS

21 January – 19 February

Aquarius

The Aquarius Personality

One fact overrides all others when considering what Aquarians are like. You have to remember that Aquarians are completely different from every other sign; something sets them apart from everyone else. To an Aquarian, this can feel like being a square peg in a round hole, and it may take years before they fit in with the people around them or even feel comfortable about being so unconformist. The typical Aquarian approaches life from a very different perspective to most people. Each Aquarian is a one-off, being completely original and innovative.

Uranus, the planetary ruler of Aquarius, is responsible for this originality. This planet works in unpredictable and erratic ways, and Aquarians feel its influence very strongly. For a start, it makes them totally independent. They follow the beat of a different drum and need to go their own way through life. Loved ones who try to stop them or hold them back will soon discover how useless this policy is – like trying to stem a flood with a paper tissue. If anything, it will make the Aquarian even more determined to do their own thing. And if no one else likes it, tough!

This is a good reminder of one of the principal Aquarian characteristics – stubbornness verging on obstinacy. Once an Aquarian has made up their mind about something, you'll go blue in the face trying to persuade them to change it. They simply aren't interested. Even if their decision is inconvenient for everyone else, or possibly even offensive, they still won't budge. This single-minded determination operates in every area of their life. However, they're very hard to predict, so even if you think you know how an Aquarian will react to something, they'll probably take you by complete surprise and do the very opposite. This is all part of the fun of knowing an Aquarian!

Usually, the present is of much more interest to an Aquarian than the past. They like to focus on the here and now, rather than get caught up in what happened a week last Wednesday. They also have their finger on the pulse of the future, which is where they really come into their own. Often an Aquarian is light years ahead of others in their thinking. As a result, they can seem like an iconoclast, possibly even a threat, because they have revolutionary theories or go against the tide of popular ideas. Not that this bothers them!

As the third of the Air signs, Aquarians operate on a predominantly mental level. This makes them extremely intelligent and tremendously rational – often to the exasperation of the people around them who tend to take a more emotional approach to life. Aquarians are capable of distancing themselves from situations so they can view them objectively. This makes them seem quite dispassionate, and possibly even heartless, but it means they don't get swept along by emotion or sentiment. Instead, they can simply deal with the facts. Well, that's their excuse, anyway!

Love

Aquarius is the friendliest sign in the zodiac, and Aquarians work hard to be chummy with everyone they meet. In fact, an Aquarian without friends feels as uncomfortable as a cow on a swing. They value their friends highly and they need to know that they're around, even if they don't get together very often.

When it comes to loving relationships, it's vital for an Aquarian to choose a lover who is also a friend. They may even realize that the most important relationships in their life begin as friendships, with love only arriving after they've established a strong platonic rapport with each other. It's very hard for an Aquarian to love someone if they don't like them too.

It's also important for an Aquarian to find a partner whose intellect matches their own, so they've always got fresh subjects to talk about and they can have long discussions about abstract ideas and concepts. The Aquarian will quickly get bored if the conversation never progresses past what was on television last night.

An Aquarian's partner must also understand and respect their need for independence. This doesn't mean the Aquarian wants to sleep with everyone they meet – they're far too loyal and honest for that – but it does mean they hate to think someone's keeping tabs on them and wants to know their every move. They would loathe the sort of relationship where they're joined at the hip to their partner and they have to do everything together. It would soon make them feel stifled and it wouldn't be long before the Aquarian called a halt to the whole arrangement. The Aquarian needs to feel that they can come and go as they like. However, it may not be quite so easy for them when the boot's on the other foot, and they may find it a struggle to give their partner the same freedom that they want themselves!

Career

An Aquarian is far too intelligent to be happy with a dead-end job where they always have one eye on the clock. They need a fulfilling career that gives them plenty to think about. Although many Aquarians do make a success of their careers, this is more by accident than design – they don't deliberately set out to become the best in their field. Instead, their wholehearted involvement and strong intellect ensures they're noticed by people who can help them make it to the top. Their streak of originality also helps to make them stand out from the crowd.

Ideally, an Aquarian's career should draw on their tremendous humanitarian instincts – they might be attracted to charity or social work, or have a job that involves fighting for the rights of the underdog. They can't stand the idea of being a 'fat cat' or living off the efforts of others, so they shy away from any job that obviously exploits people or that goes against their strong principles. However, they aren't averse to making money if they think they've earned it!

Being self-employed is ideal for an Aquarian because they'll thrive as their own boss. They have all the motivation and determination needed to ensure they get the work done in time. Self-employment brings other benefits because an Aquarian often has problems when dealing with authority figures. Being confronted by someone in charge often brings out the Aquarian's rebellious streak! And it's even worse if they think the person in authority doesn't know what they're doing or is only in it for the money. It's not easy for an Aquarian to take orders from other people, generally because they think they could do their job so much better. And they're probably absolutely right!

Money

Aquarians are happy to talk about most subjects but this is one topic that can make them feel uncomfortable. They have a love–hate relationship with money. Although they know that they need money to live, and they relish occasional bouts of extravagance, they hate the way this sucks them into a consumer-led society. For instance, although they appreciate the labour-saving qualities of washing machines, a part of them hates the idea of owning one because it turns them into a consumer just like everyone else.

Aquarians also loathe the idea of making money for its own sake. Provided they have enough to keep a roof over their head and food on their plate, why should they need a lot of cash in the bank? Unfortunately this attitude doesn't always go down very well with partners and family members because it can lead to misunderstanding and resentment, especially if everyone suspects the Aquarian is out of touch with the cost of living. A partner may even feel that they've been saddled with the responsibility of being the main breadwinner, while the Aquarian has a whale of a time doing whatever they want.

Humanitarianism runs through an Aquarian like letters through a stick of seaside rock, and they are usually happy to help out anyone in financial trouble. Yet very often charity begins at home for them. The Aquarian may make a point of never giving to charity because they say the charities don't spend the money on the right things, but they will happily bail out a friend or relative who's up against it.

Although an Aquarian will keep a close eye on the day-to-day management of their bank account, they're not very interested in high finance and will be happy with a moderate savings account. They detest the thought of getting rich by investing in large companies whose business practices are harming the environment or exploiting people. Aquarians have high and uncompromising standards on such matters.

Health

Because an Aquarian's energies tend to operate in an erratic way, it's very important for them to take steady and regular exercise. Alternating long periods of inactivity with sweaty bursts of exertion is a recipe for disaster. Besides which, pounding away in the gym or jogging through fume-filled streets isn't an Aquarian's idea of fun – quite frankly, they can't see the point of it. Far better to find an activity that allows them to exercise their body and relax their mind at the same time – something like yoga, Pilates or Qi Gong is ideal. They also benefit from meditation, especially if they can do it with other people.

An Aquarian understands the importance of eating a healthy diet and is probably very sympathetic towards the idea of vegetarianism, if not veganism too. Organic foods also appeal to them and they may even grow their own organic fruit and vegetables. Other special diets, such as food-combining or macrobiotics, can attract them and will suit their sensitive system. However, it's important that the Aquarian doesn't become so stubborn and dogmatic about this that they refuse to relax the rules when they're being entertained by other people and thereby cause offence. They can also become unwell if they follow an extreme diet. When they are ill, they may respond well to complementary medicine because they like the holistic approach that's involved.

An Aquarian's circulation and ankles are the two most vulnerable areas of their body. They should make sure their ankles are well-supported whenever they exercise, and choose shoes and boots that fit their feet properly. Regular exercise will help keep their circulation working efficiently.

The World of Aquarius

Cities	Bremen, Hamburg, Salzburg, Stockholm
Countries	Canada, Ethiopia, Poland, Sweden
Colour	Electric blue
Number	Eleven
Day of the week	Saturday
Gemstone	Aquamarine
Crystal	Peridot
Animal	Bird
Foods	Kiwi fruit, prickly pear, star fruit
Plants	Apple tree, orchid, Solomon's seal
Tarot card	The Star

Compatibility

Aquarius with Aries

This combination is good fun, especially as friends. Neither sign is scared to say what they think, so they'll have some good-humoured but fierce debates. The only real snag comes if the Aquarian's emotions are too cool for the hot-blooded Arien. The Aquarian may also be charmed at first, and then irritated, by the Arien's naïveté.

Aquarius with Taurus

This couple will struggle to stay together as they have so little in common. They also have very different ways of looking at the world. The Aquarian will soon be frustrated by the Taurean's need to cling to the status quo, and will feel bemused by the Taurean's slightly possessive attitude. Why can't they lighten up? the Aquarian wonders.

Aquarius with Gemini

Whatever the nature of this couple's relationship, it will have a strongly intellectual slant. They'll love talking about virtually every subject under the sun, and the Aquarian will teach the Gemini to think things through in more detail and without leaping to easy conclusions. Both of them benefit from this alliance.

Aquarius with Cancer

This is a mystifying pairing. It's hard to imagine what will bring them together in the first place, let alone keep them together! The Aquarian will soon tire of the way the Cancerian lives on their emotions, and will feel suffocated by the care and attention that's lavished on them. They must make plenty of allowances for each other.

Aquarius with Leo

This is great fun! The Aquarian admires the Leo's style and self-confidence, although they find it hard to cope with their tendency to turn a snag into a drama. Emotionally, they have a lot to learn from the affectionate Leo, who will encourage them to be more open about their feelings and more demonstrative.

Aquarius with Virgo

As friends, this couple have plenty of differences but they can surmount them. As lovers, they could quickly come unstuck. Neither sign is renowned for being emotional and this is where problems start. Their relationship could soon become rather distant and sterile, with neither of them knowing how to bridge the gap.

Aquarius with Libra

This is one of the best combinations for an Aquarian. They marvel at the Libran's tact, enjoy their considerate nature and appreciate their agile brain. They will also enjoy teasing the Libran and watching them rise to the bait! This couple are great friends, good business partners and happy lovers, so they win all round.

Aquarius with Scorpio

What do you get when you put two of the most dogmatic signs together? Stalemate! Differences of opinion will spring up all the time, with neither person wanting to back down. Problems over the Aquarian's need for independence will drive a wedge between them, with the Aquarian feeling trapped and manipulated.

Aquarius with Sagittarius

Here are two people who both need to go their own way,

but there's no danger of them drifting apart – the very fact that their partner gives them plenty of scope will keep them together. They'll enjoy fascinating conversations because neither sign is a dunce. They will also share a deep love for one another, based on mutual respect.

Aquarius with Capricorn

Give and take is needed on both sides if this relationship is to work. The iconoclastic Aquarian must appreciate the Capricorn's conservative attitude, and the Capricorn must learn to relax more. They're great as business partners because their combined gifts create an unstoppable team. But as lovers, they don't know what to make of each other.

Aquarius with Aquarius

This could be a marriage of true minds or it could be a recipe for disaster! Provided each Aquarian is willing to listen to their partner, their relationship will flourish. But if each one insists that only their opinion counts and their partner is talking rubbish, they will be heading for trouble. Sexually, it will be great or gruesome.

Aquarius with Pisces

This relationship has all the makings of a mismatch. The Aquarian can't understand why the Piscean is so sensitive and easily hurt, and the Piscean thinks the Aquarian is so strange they must have come from another planet. They aren't natural friends but they'll eventually forge a bond. A love affair, however, will be much harder work.

PISCES

20 February – 20 March

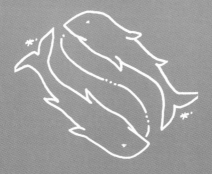

Pisces

The Pisces Personality

Pisces is the last of the twelve signs of the zodiac and it's said to contain a little of each of the other eleven signs. Some people even believe that a soul's last incarnation is always under the sign of Pisces. No one knows whether that's true, but Pisces is certainly the sign of the saint or the sinner – or both rolled into one. The symbol, or glyph, for Pisces represents two fish swimming in opposite directions, and this describes the way Pisces can hit the heights or sink to the lowest depths. It's a sign of extremes.

It can be very difficult for a Piscean to keep their feet on the ground, so they often come across as someone who is other-worldly and possibly even completely flaky. This is because they are ruled by the mystical, spiritual planet Neptune. And their Water element means they are easily swayed by their emotions.

The result is that Pisces is the sign of the dreamer, the visionary and the saint, but it can also be the sign of the fantasist and the criminal, thanks to Neptune's boundless capacity for escapism and deception. Some Pisceans can talk themselves into almost anything.

One of the most outstanding characteristics of a typical Piscean is their kindness. They have an almost bottomless reservoir of compassion for other people, even when they suspect they are being conned by them. Many Pisceans will work hard for their favourite charity or for a local good cause, although you may never know anything about it because they don't like advertising their good works.

Many Pisceans say they go through life in a dream. As teenagers they don't have a chosen career and they feel they drift from one situation to another, almost at the mercy of whatever fate has to offer them. They can be like pieces of seaweed floating with the tide.

Something else that's very noticeable about a Piscean is their capacity to show emotion. They are easily moved to tears and may even be unable to watch news programmes because they can't bear to see so much suffering.

Pisceans struggle to face up to harsh reality. They have an instinctive dislike of unpleasant situations or harsh facts, and try to put as much distance between these and themselves as possible. This may simply mean that they're reluctant to watch violent films or read unsavoury articles in the newspapers, or it may make them view life through rose-coloured glasses, ultimately deceiving themselves into believing things are much better than they really are. The results of this tactic can be disastrous, because it means they can turn a blind eye to trouble until it's unavoidable – and too late to do anything about it. If a Piscean wants to be truly happy, they must learn to temper their need for peace and harmony with an ability to face up to life as it really is, warts and all.

Love

It is a rare Piscean who can separate their emotions from their daily life. Instead, they usually have an emotional reaction to everything and everyone they encounter. And they can't do much about it – it's simply the way they operate.

A Piscean often wears their heart on their sleeve, and what a huge heart they have! This makes them a born romantic but also very sensitive and vulnerable to possible hurt and pain. Sometimes, they may even see slights where none exist, or allow their imagination to work overtime so they dream up an entire incident with someone. It also means they are extremely emotional, and they pour out love and affection to their favourite people. If the Piscean is lucky, their loved ones are able to respond in kind or to accept their love without feeling overwhelmed. Even so, the Piscean should try to keep their feelings in check if they threaten to spiral out of control too often. Some signs simply can't cope with a lot of highly-charged drama and the Piscean will feel hurt if their partner tunes out – especially if that happens to be in the middle of a crisis.

Most Pisceans are faithful but you might meet one who has several partners on the go at one time. These Pisceans have a tremendous capacity for deception (not that they see it that way, of course), and they seem so thoroughly nice that no one would suspect they're busy juggling their string of lovers. It's all part of the Piscean duality.

It's natural for a Piscean to see the best in other people, which is one of the reasons they have so many admirers. However, it also puts the Piscean at risk of potential heartbreak because it makes them blind to a loved one's failings. Even if everyone else can see that their latest love is no good for them, the Piscean will persist in ignoring their faults and trusting that love will find a way. When it does, they're deliriously happy. When it doesn't, they sink to the depths of despair.

Career

The dual Piscean nature really comes into its own here. This sign is drawn to professions that are either incredibly glamorous and artistic or which involve being of service to others and are therefore incredibly unglamorous!

The film industry is ruled by Neptune, the ruler of Pisces, and many members of this sign are photographers, actors, dancers, choreographers and designers. Pisceans are also attracted to the perfumery, cosmetics and fashion businesses. Neptune rules alcohol too, so you'll find many Pisceans running drinking clubs and pubs, or working in breweries. They may also be involved in the oil industry.

Many Pisceans devote their lives to looking after others, especially in institutions such as hospitals, hospices and prisons. They have the capacity to be completely self-sacrificing and they will cheerfully do all sorts of menial jobs. The contemplative life of a religious order can also appeal to Pisceans, who enjoy living very simply and devoting their life to God. At the other extreme, there are plenty of Pisceans living on the wrong side of the law, possibly involved in smuggling, dealing drugs and other illicit activities. Pisceans really do span the whole range of human behaviour!

Wherever a Piscean works, they need a sympathetic atmosphere, pleasant surroundings and colleagues who understand and appreciate them. Any job where they're nothing more than a drudge will quickly depress them and may eventually make them ill. Pisces is one of the most creative signs of all, so ideally a Piscean should be able to express this side of their nature even if only in a small way. They also have a powerful imagination which needs a constructive outlet, otherwise it might play games with them. If they can't put these artistic gifts to use in their job, they should make sure they express them in their spare time, otherwise they will soon feel very frustrated.

Money

Pisces and money go together like oil and water, especially when it comes to the day-to-day management of a Piscean's finances. Very often, they don't have a clue whether they're in the red or rolling in money. A typical Piscean concentrates most of their energy on creative activities rather than materialistic ones, so their heart probably plummets every time they think about their finances. They may find it difficult to keep track of where all the money goes, or might get into a real state whenever it's time to tackle their taxes (the very thought of which probably makes them feel sick). The best answer to this is either to pay a trustworthy accountant to handle their finances for them, if they can afford it, or to grit their teeth and tackle things sooner rather than later so there is no need for panics and crises.

Although a Piscean is prone at times to dreaming of a wonderfully lavish lifestyle, they are probably perfectly happy if they have enough money to live on, preferably with a little left over to give to their loved ones. All the same, it's a good idea for them to set aside any spare cash for a rainy day or a big treat, but they should make sure they get sound, independent financial advice before doing this. Because most Pisceans are so trusting, it's easy for sharks and con men to get the better of them, so they should be very cautious when investing their money and make sure they aren't talked into taking risks they can't afford.

If a Piscean happens to be rich, they like to live in the most luxurious and extravagant way possible. They'll be able to live out all their fantasies, and one of the first items on their shopping list will be their own personal swimming pool. A private yacht wouldn't go amiss, either!

Health

Emotions and health often go hand in hand, and a Piscean's well-being can be powerfully affected by their feelings. If they are unhappy, it can show in their body, perhaps through a chill or a cold. Stress can present particular problems for a Piscean because it can play havoc with their finely tuned nervous system, triggering such symptoms as headaches, stomach upsets and sleepless nights. It's important for a Piscean to take immense care of themselves, making sure they don't skimp on meals and that they get plenty of rest. Whenever they feel particularly vulnerable they should try to keep away from tense or unpleasant atmospheres because they can absorb negative vibrations like a psychic sponge. They may even find that they come out in sympathy whenever someone describes their illness, so they should be especially wary of people who've always got a tale of woe to tell because they'll affect the Piscean deeply.

The feet are the most vulnerable area of the body for a Piscean, so they may suffer from corns, chilblains or struggle to find shoes that fit properly. Whenever they become tense, they'll feel better if they treat themselves to a pedicure or give themselves a foot massage, which will help to clear any build-up of negative energy. Walking on grass with bare feet can help to ground them. Swimming is perfect for them and is a marvellous way for them to combine exercise and relaxation. They may be allergic to certain foods or drugs, and may respond much better to complementary medicines than some prescription drugs.

The World of Pisces

Cities	Alexandria, Seville, Warsaw
Countries	Egypt, Portugal, Scandinavia
Colours	Sea green, turquoise
Number	Nine
Day of the week	Thursday
Gemstone	Aquamarine
Crystal	Chrysolite
Animal	Fish
Foods	Cucumber, pumpkin, watercress
Plants	Fig tree, waterlily, willow tree
Tarot card	The Moon

Compatibility

Pisces with Aries

Despite initial fascination between two people who are profoundly different, this relationship will struggle to survive. There is simply too big a gap between them. They are much happier as friends than lovers because the Arien will soon become frustrated with the dreamy Piscean who prefers romance to raunchy lust.

Pisces with Taurus

There's a lot of mutual empathy and understanding in this relationship. They have a similar approach to life and love because they both crave emotional security. However, the Piscean may sometimes find the Taurean is rather too literal and prosaic for their taste, but they may be able to encourage them to be more imaginative in time.

Pisces with Gemini

Ideally, this couple should be friends or business partners rather than lovers. Although they have many interests in common, their emotional needs are so different that these will soon lead to misunderstandings. The Piscean wishes the Gemini were more demonstrative and less scared of showing their feelings, but may be unable to say so.

Pisces with Cancer

These are two of the most sensitive signs of the zodiac so they feel safe when they get together. At least they know they won't be deliberately hurt. In fact, they may go out of their way to protect each other's feelings, and this may lead to hitches if they feel incapable of talking problems through in case they upset the apple cart.

Pisces with Leo

This is an uneasy combination and definitely one that stands a better chance of success if it's platonic rather than passionate. The Piscean will adore helping the Leo to enjoy the good life but after a while they may feel rather harried by the Leo's tendency to organize them and boss them about. This is less likely to happen if they're just friends.

Pisces with Virgo

Opposites usually attract but in this case they can repel. At first, the Piscean likes the Virgo's no-nonsense attitude and ability to bail them out of trouble, but after a while it can start to grate. They may even unconsciously become more disorganized in order to annoy the Virgo! They will also feel hurt by the Virgo's nagging and criticism.

Pisces with Libra

It's romance all the way when these two get together. They will put a lot of effort into keeping their relationship as fresh and exciting as when it began. However, this can cause problems if neither person wants to face up to the inevitable difficulties that arise in any relationship. They both have to be prepared to tackle the bad times as well as the good.

Pisces with Scorpio

Emotion flows thick and fast between this couple. As friends, they'll talk for hours about their relationships and swap war stories. As lovers, they'll enjoy a partnership that seethes with drama and sizzles with sensation. Everything will be conducted at a heightened level, which is exactly the way both of them like it.

Pisces with Sagittarius

This works as a friendship because these people have enough in common to keep them talking for hours. They may also share a religious or spiritual quest. But things can get dicey if they fall in love because there is so much scope for crossed wires and hurt feelings, with the Piscean bearing the brunt of the pain.

Pisces with Capricorn

Although they seem like chalk and cheese, this couple manage to get on well together, provided the Piscean isn't too unworldly. The Piscean admires the Capricorn's head for business and their capacity for hard work, and the Capricorn likes the Piscean's sensitivity. They will both do their best to make their home a cosy and safe place.

Pisces with Aquarius

These people come from different worlds and can't make head nor tail of each other. They will manage as friends, although it will take a lot of spade work to reach that point, but will encounter many problems in an emotional relationship. Their needs are so dissimilar that they will struggle to understand one another.

Pisces with Pisces

This is a great partnership because neither Piscean has to explain themselves to anyone. Sometimes there may even be no need for words because there is such a depth of shared understanding. Yet this can lead to sticky patches because both Pisceans will allow their imagination to run away with them if they don't have the facts.

Further Reading

The following books are all good introductions to the fascinating world of astrology. Some of them deal solely with Sun signs, others take you further into the astrological realms.

Carole Golder, *Astrology*, Piatkus Books, 1999

Linda Goodman, *Linda Goodman's Love Signs*, Pan Books, 1980

Linda Goodman, *Linda Goodman's Relationship Signs*, Macmillan, 1998

Linda Goodman, *Linda Goodman's Sun Signs*, Pan Books, 1972

Liz Greene, *Astrology for Lovers*, Thorsons, 1999

Charles and Suzi Harvey, *The Principles of Astrology*, Thorsons, 1998

Charles and Suzi Harvey, *Sun Sign, Moon Sign*, Thorsons, 1994

Julia and Derek Parker, *Parker's Astrology*, Dorling Kindersley, 1991

Astrology Websites

The Internet is changing all the time, with new websites appearing and old ones vanishing or turning into something else. This is a selection of astrology websites that are worth visiting and which offer a wide range of information. Many of them include links to other sites.

www.astrology.about.com/science/astrology
From the simple to the esoteric, this site also offers chart calculation.

www.astrology.com
This offers horoscopes, basic astrological information and features on love and career.

www.astro-horoscopes.net
This site is aimed at beginners as well as more experienced astrologers. It has information on astrological software and organizations.

www.astrology-numerology.com
A comprehensive website offering a good introduction to the nuts and bolts of astrology. As its title suggests, it also features numerology.

www.AstrologyZine.com

This site is packed with information, including horoscopes, teach-yourself astrology and many articles.

www.astronet.women.com

A fun site offering horoscopes, plus personal astrological and tarot readings.

www.thezodiac.com

An exciting site that takes you further than Sun signs.